Praise for *Tidy First?*

Kent Beck is always worth listening to, and I have been waiting for the advice in this book for several decades now. This book helps to move the focus in software away from the tools and technology, and firmly onto what really matters, design! Design is about the shapes we paint with our code, and Kent helps us to paint better shapes. This is an important book on an important topic.

—Dave Farley,
Founder and Director of Continuous Delivery Ltd.

With code bases that are hard to understand, it can be difficult for a developer to know where to start. This book gives practical tips for a developer at any level to help improve the code they work with.

—Sam Newman, independent consultant, technologist, and
author of Building Microservices *and* Monolith to Microservices

Kent Beck shares dozens of easy-to-follow ideas on how to turn complicated code into a simpler form. The ideas are simple, and yet, as you read them, you will wonder why you haven't thought about many of these before. Recommended for anyone who cares about clean and readable code.

—Gergely Orosz, The Pragmatic Engineer

For decades, refactoring books have focused on top-down, object-oriented software design theories. *Tidy First?* breaks the mold by providing a realistic approach to incrementally improving real production code.

—Maude Lemaire, author of Refactoring at Scale

Let's be honest: 99% of a software engineer's job involves working on brownfield projects. This can be difficult, especially if the code wasn't written with readability in mind. In this book, Kent Beck turns things around by prioritizing human relationships through code. He succinctly teaches how to improve software design with small, gradual changes, thereby making the code clearer for both you and your colleagues.

—*Vlad Khononov, author of* Learning Domain-Driven Design

Tidy First?
A Personal Exercise in Empirical Software Design

Kent Beck

Foreword by Larry Constantine

Beijing · Boston · Farnham · Sebastopol · Tokyo

Tidy First?

by Kent Beck

Copyright © 2024 Kent Beck. All rights reserved.

Published by O'Reilly Media, Inc., 1005 Gravenstein Highway North, Sebastopol, CA 95472.

O'Reilly books may be purchased for educational, business, or sales promotional use. Online editions are also available for most titles (*http://oreilly.com*). For more information, contact our corporate/institutional sales department: 800-998-9938 or *corporate@oreilly.com*.

Acquisitions Editors: Melissa Duffield, Louise Corrigan	**Proofreader:** Piper Editorial Consulting, LLC
Development Editor: Michele Cronin	**Indexer:** nSight, Inc.
Production Editor: Christopher Faucher	**Interior Designer:** David Futato
Copyeditor: Rachel Head	**Cover Designer:** Karen Montgomery
	Illustrator: Kate Dullea

October 2023:   First Edition

Revision History for the First Edition

2023-10-17:   First Release

See *http://oreilly.com/catalog/errata.csp?isbn=9781098151249* for release details.

978-1-098-15124-9

[LSI]

To the blessed memory of Professor Barry Dwolatzky:
geek extraordinaire, elemental force, and inspiration.

Table of Contents

Part II.   Managing

Part III.   Theory

Foreword

This slim volume, the first of a series, is for professional programmers–that breed of software developers with a deep and geeky interest in their craft and in improving their work in small ways with big payoffs. The author, Kent Beck, is just such a dedicated professional, ever attentive to detail and ever in tune with the larger issues and the bigger picture.

Practicing software developers often pay scant attention to theory, but Kent knows what he is talking about when he mixes practice and theory into a guide to tidy code that is both readable and practical.

In theory, there is no difference between theory and practice, while in practice there is. Various versions of this pithy pronouncement have been widely and incorrectly attributed to Albert Einstein and Yogi Berra, among others. Only a nerdy wordsmith (guilty as charged!) would care that the correct attribution is to Benjamin Brewster, a student at Yale writing in an 1882 edition of the *Yale Literary Magazine*. Thanks to the dedicated word geeks at QuoteInvestigator.com, I can offer this bit of geeky detail confident of the audience here: this is a profession that hinges on getting the details right.

In bringing theory and practice together, Kent starts at the bottom, with tiny snippets of code and meticulous attention to small details, then works his way up to the larger view that explains the process of creating cleaner code that is more robust in the face of inevitable changes and corrections. In assembling this guide to practice, Kent ultimately draws on the real-world economics of software development along with core theory in software engineering.

That core theory is simply this: that the complexity of computer code depends on how it is organized into parts, on how coupled those parts are with each other and on how cohesive the parts are in themselves. The source of the theory of coupling and cohesion is usually attributed to my book with Ed Yourdon, *Structured Design* (Yourdon Press, 1975; Prentice Hall, 1979), although it can be traced all the way back to a 1968 conference presentation in Cambridge, Massachusetts. Coupling and cohesion almost didn't make it into the 1979 Prentice Hall edition. The editors tried to convince Ed and I to omit the two chapters because "no one is interested in theory." Fortunately for the history of software engineering, the authors prevailed and the editors were proved wrong. The theory has since been validated through a half century of practice and literally hundreds of research studies and investigations.

Coupling and cohesion are simply measures of the complexity of computer code, not from the perspective of the computers executing the programs but that of human beings trying to understand the code. To understand any program, whether to create it or to correct it or to change it, requires understanding the piece of code immediately in front of you as well as those other pieces to which it is connected, which it depends on or affects or is affected by. It is easier to understand the immediate piece of code if it all hangs together, if it makes sense as a whole, if it forms what cognitive psychologists call a gestalt. That's cohesion. It is also easier to understand it in terms of its relationships with other pieces of code if these relationships are few and relatively weak or highly constrained. That's coupling. Coupling and cohesion are really all about how your brain deals with complicated systems.

See? Nice and tidy. That's the theory. Now on to the practical details and the mix with just enough theory to make sense of it all. Kent Beck will ably guide you on the way.

— Larry Constantine
Rowley, Massachusetts
9 October 2023

Larry Constantine is a former professor at the University of Madeira, Portugal, and the University of Technology, Sydney, Australia. He has more than 200 papers and three dozen books to his credit, including the Jolt Award winner, *Software for Use* (Addison Wesley, 1999), written with Lucy Lockwood, and fifteen novels under his pen name, Lior Samson.

Preface

What Is Tidy First?

"I have to change this code, but it's messy. What should I do first?"

"Maybe I should tidy the code before I make the change. Maybe. Some. Or maybe not?"

These are questions you might ask yourself, and if there were easy answers, I wouldn't have felt the need to write a book to address them.

Tidy First? describes:

- When to tidy messy code before changing what it computes
- How to tidy messy code safely and efficiently
- How to stop tidying messy code
- Why tidying works

Software design is an exercise in human relationships. In *Tidy First?* we start with the proverbial person in the mirror—with the programmer's relationship with themself. Why don't we take time to care for ourselves? Take time to make our work easier? Why do we go down the rabbit hole of cleaning code to the exclusion of work that would help our users?

Tidy First? is the next step in my mission to help geeks feel safe in the world. It's also the first step to take when faced with messy code. Software design is a powerful tool to ease pain in the world—if it is used well. Used badly, it becomes just another instrument of oppression, and a drag on the effectiveness of software development.

Tidy First? is the first of a series of books focusing on software design. I want to make software design approachable and valued, so I'm starting with the kind of software design you can do on your own. Subsequent volumes will apply software design to heal relationships between the programmers on a team, and then address the biggie:

the relationship between business and technology. But first, let's understand and practice software design in ways that benefit our daily work.

Let's say you have a big function containing many lines of code. Before changing it, you read that code to understand what is going on. In the process, you see how you can logically divide the code into smaller chunks. When you extract those chunks, you're tidying. Other kinds of tidying include using guard clauses, explaining comments, and helper functions.

As a book, *Tidy First?* practices what it proposes—delivering these *tidyings* in small chunks and suggesting when and where you might apply them. So, instead of trying to master tidying all at once, you can try out a few tidyings that make sense for your problem. *Tidy First?* also begins describing the theory behind software design: coupling, cohesion, discounted cash flows, and optionality.

Audience

This book is meant for programmers, lead developers, hands-on software architects, and technical managers. It is not tied to any programming language, and all developers will be able to read and apply the concepts in this book to their own projects. This book assumes that the reader is not new to programming in general.

What You Will Learn

By the end of this book, you will understand:

- The fundamental difference between changes to the behavior of a system and changes to its structure
- The enabling magic of alternating investment in structure and investment in behavior, as a lone programmer changing code
- The basics of the theory of how software design works and the forces that act on it

And you will be able to:

- Improve your own experience of programming by sometimes tidying first (and sometimes tidying after).
- Begin to make large changes in small, safe steps.
- Prepare to design as a human activity with diverging incentives.

Structure of the Book

Tidy First? is divided into an Introduction and three parts:

Introduction
> I begin with a brief description of my motivations for writing this book, how I came to write it, who it's intended for, and what you can expect. Then we dive right in.

Part I, "Tidyings"
> A tidying is like a little baby miniature refactoring. Each short chapter is a tidying. If you see code like this, then change it to code like that. Then send it to production.

Part II, "Managing"
> Next we cover managing the tidying process. Part of the tidying philosophy is that it should never be a big deal. It's never something that has to be reported, tracked, planned, and scheduled. You need to change this code, and it's hard to change because it's messy, so you tidy first. Even as part of daily business, this is still a process that improves with thought.

Part III, "Theory"
> Here's where I finally get to spread my wings and dig deep into the topics that excite me. What do I mean by "software design is an exercise in human relationships"? Who are these humans? How are their needs better met with better software design? Why does software cost so damn much? What can we do about it (spoiler alert: software design)? Coupling? Cohesion? Power laws?

My goal is for readers to begin reading in the morning and be designing better that afternoon. Then designing a little better every day after that. Pretty soon software design will no longer be the weakest link in the chain of delivering value with software.

Why "Empirical" Software Design?

The loud debates in software design seem to be about *what* to design:

- How big should services be?
- How big should repositories be?
- Events versus explicit service invocation.
- Objects versus functions versus imperative code.

These *what* debates hide a more fundamental disagreement among software designers: *when*? Here's a caricature of the poles of this disagreement:

Speculative design

> We know what we want to do next, so let's design for it today. It will be cheaper to design now. Besides, once the software is in production we will never have the chance to design, so let's pile it all in today.

Reactive design

> Features are all anyone cares about, so let's design as little as we can today so we can get back to features. Only when features become nearly impossible to add will we begrudgingly improve the design, and then only just enough to get back to features.

I aspire to answer the question of "when?" with "somewhere in the middle." When we observe that a certain class of features is hard to add, we design until the pressure is relieved. We start with just enough design to get the feedback cycles going:

Features

> What do users want?

Design

> How can programmers best be supported to deliver those features?

The empirical software design answer to the question of *when* is contingent. Design some time around when you can take advantage of the design. Answering this question requires taste, negotiation, and judgment. Is requiring taste and judgment a weakness? Sure, but it's an inevitable weakness. Speculative and reactive design also require judgment, but they give software designers fewer tools to work with.

I like the word *empirical* to describe this style because it seems to clarify the distinction I'm making with speculative and reactive design timings. "Based on, concerned with, or verifiable by observation or experience rather than theory or pure logic." Sounds about right.

How I Came to Write *Tidy First?*

As an undergraduate I took a course on software design that used the book *Structured Design* by Ed Yourdon (RIP) and Larry Constantine. I didn't understand much of the book, mostly because I hadn't yet encountered the problems it addressed.

Fast-forward 25 years to 2005. I had designed a bunch of software by this time. I felt like I had a pretty good grasp on design. Stephen Fraser organized a panel at OOPSLA (the big object-oriented programming conference) to celebrate the 30th anniversary of the publication of the book. Ed and Larry were to be on the panel, along with Rebecca Wirfs-Brock, Grady Booch, Steve McConnell, and Brian Henderson-Sellers.

If I didn't want to get blown off the stage, I had some homework to do. So I cracked open my yellowing copy of *Structured Design* and started reading. Hours later I looked up, absolutely enthralled. Here were Newton's laws of motion, but for software design. It was all so clear when it came out. How did we as an industry forget that clarity?

I remember the panel going well. A highlight of the conference was breakfast with Ed and Larry, two extremely bright guys completely comfortable with themselves and each other. Figure P-1 shows the signatures they left in my textbook long ago.

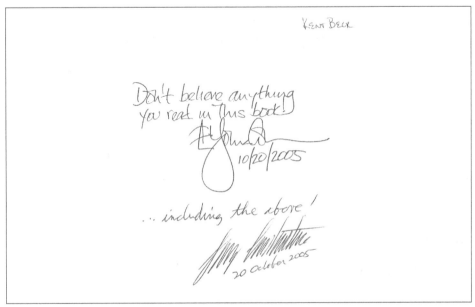

Figure P-1. Inscriptions by Ed Yourdon ("Don't believe anything you read in this book!") and Larry Constantine ("…including the above!")

The book was showing its age by that time. Examples using paper tape and magnetic tape were no longer relevant. Nor was the discussion of assembly language versus the new higher-level languages. The basics, though, were spot on. I vowed that I would bring that material to today's audience.

I made several abortive attempts to write a software design book in the intervening years (search for "Kent Beck Responsive Design" if you want to see what I was up to). It wasn't until 2019 that I unexpectedly had two weeks of completely unscheduled time. I decided to see how much of the book I could write in those two weeks.

Ten thousand words later, I had learned an important lesson—I wasn't going to be able to tackle all of software design in one book. One scenario that kept coming up in what I had drafted was this moment of small-scale design: I have some messy code—do I change it or do I tidy it first?

My book-writing experience has always been like this. Take a topic that seems too small for a book. Write. Discover the topic is way too large for a book. Take a tiny, too-small slice. Write. Discover the slice is too large. Repeat.

And so here you hold (virtually or for real) the first fruits of that now nearly 20-year-old vow. I found that in discussing that hourly question, "Should I tidy first?" I have been able to touch on many of the topics dear to my designer heart. I look forward to your feedback and to continuing to deepen my understanding of all that makes software design fun and valuable.

O'Reilly Online Learning

 For more than 40 years, *O'Reilly Media* has provided technology and business training, knowledge, and insight to help companies succeed.

Our unique network of experts and innovators share their knowledge and expertise through books, articles, and our online learning platform. O'Reilly's online learning platform gives you on-demand access to live training courses, in-depth learning paths, interactive coding environments, and a vast collection of text and video from O'Reilly and 200+ other publishers. For more information, visit *https://oreilly.com*.

How to Contact Us

Please address comments and questions concerning this book to the publisher:

O'Reilly Media, Inc.
1005 Gravenstein Highway North
Sebastopol, CA 95472
800-889-8969 (in the United States or Canada)
707-829-7019 (international or local)
707-829-0104 (fax)
support@oreilly.com
https://www.oreilly.com/about/contact.html

We have a web page for this book, where we list errata, examples, and any additional information. You can access this page at *https://oreil.ly/tidy-first*.

Email *bookquestions@oreilly.com* to comment or ask technical questions about this book.

For news and information about our books and courses, visit *https://oreilly.com*.

Find us on LinkedIn: *https://linkedin.com/company/oreilly-media*

Follow us on Twitter: *https://twitter.com/oreillymedia*

Watch us on YouTube: *https://youtube.com/oreillymedia*

Acknowledgments

The "author" of a book is an accounting fiction. I typed the words, but *these* words wouldn't be in your hands without a host of people. Here are some.

Thanks for early technical feedback to Anna Goodman, Matan Zruya, Jeff Carbonella, David Haley, Kelly Sutton, and the rest of my students at Gusto. Thanks for technical feedback on the manuscript to Maude Lemaire, Rebecca Wirfs-Brock, Vlad Khononov, and Oleksii Torunov. Thanks to my paying subscribers on *https://tidy first.substack.com* for giving me the gift of time to write and for their feedback on the chapters as I drafted them.

Thanks to the expert production team at O'Reilly, who made the process as smooth as it can possibly be: Melissa Duffield, Michele Cronin, Louise Corrigan. Thanks to Tim O'Reilly for taking a chance on a short book.

Thanks to Keith Adams and Pamela Vagata for technical talk, encouragement, and the occasional cocktail. Thanks to Susan for the right mix of encouragement and nudging. Thanks to my children, Beth, Lincoln, Lindsey, Forrest, and Joëlle.

Thanks to my software design mentors and colleagues: Ward Cunningham, Martin Fowler, Ron Jeffries, Erich Gamma, David Saff, and Massimo Arnoldi.

Finally, thanks to Ed Yourdan (of blessed memory) and Larry Constantine for figuring all this stuff out so long ago.

Introduction

Software design is a sharp tool. Some folks don't know they wield it. Some folks who wield it grab it by the blade, not the handle. That's one big reason why I'm writing about software design. It goes back to my personal mission statement: help geeks feel safe in the world.

That mission cuts two ways. Sometimes geeks design software in unsafe ways, ways that accidentally break the behavior of the system, or ways that strain the human relationships supporting the software. It's sensible to feel unsafe when you're acting unsafe. It's far better to feel unsafe when you're acting unsafe than it is to feel blithely, cluelessly safe.

Helping folks learn to design safely contributes to my mission. Hence, you will see frequent references to working in small, safe steps throughout these pages. I'm not interested in short-term acceleration. Software design creates value, when it creates value, that is realized over time.

Tidy first is a bit of an exception. When you tidy first, you know you will realize the value of tidying immediately. This is a setup. I want you to get used to manipulating the structure of your code just as much as you manipulate its behavior. As we get further into design, we'll talk about actions with longer- and longer-term payoff, actions that affect more people.

When I've read other descriptions of software design, I've found them to be missing the critical elements of "how much?" and "when?" Other software designers seemed to act like design took place out of time, either before you had any of that pesky code to slow you down or in an indefinite time-out from the ongoing pressure to change the behavior of the code. I wanted to explore those questions, and see if I could provide useful principles for answering them.

Software design has always offered me an intellectual puzzle. I enjoy the moment of wondering, "What is the design which, if I had it, would shrink this big change into a bite-sized morsel?" For me, there is a whiff of sadism in programming, a heroic self-immolation on the pyre of complexity. The world is challenging enough that we can't afford to ignore opportunities to make things easier for ourselves and others.

Another aspect of the puzzle of software design is figuring out what forces drive it, and what principles to use to respond to those forces. Much design advice just flat-out contradicts the available evidence. Why is it that skilled designers produce results that can't possibly proceed from the principles they espouse? What's really going on?

A book offers nowhere to hide. If I don't understand some topic fully, you'll know, and there's nothing I can do about that. An example is cohesion—a concept I could crisply define 15 years ago but couldn't satisfactorily explain until last year. I want to push myself to understand.

Avalanches are the best. There's a particular moment I hope you'll get to as you practice tidying first. You tidy this bit that makes this feature easier. That bit that makes that feature easier. Then the tidyings start to compound. Because you made this easier, that becomes easier. Suddenly, without you ever straining, a giant simplification becomes the matter of a stroke or two of your pen. And because you brought your colleagues along every step of the way, you have a totally informed audience for your genius; an audience that becomes more appreciative as it, too, begins to harvest the benefits of your little-little-then-big structure change.

I'll finish my list of motivations with finances. As I've written elsewhere, I don't write to make money; I make money with writing so I can afford to write. As with all technical books, I don't expect a jackpot payoff from these books. If it means I can afford a better car, that's plenty to encourage me to write instead of painting, playing guitar, or playing poker. So yes, I want to make a little coin with this, but I intend to offer far more value than I charge.

PART I

Tidyings

My general learning strategy is to go from concrete to abstract. Therefore, we'll start with a catalog of little design "moves" you can make when faced with messy code you have to change.

Those of you familiar with refactoring will see great similarity between refactorings, defined as changes to structure that don't change behavior, and tidyings. Tidyings are a subset of refactorings. Tidyings are the cute, fuzzy little refactorings that nobody could possibly hate on.

"Refactoring" took fatal damage when folks started using it to refer to long pauses in feature development. They even eliminated the "that don't change behavior" clause, so "refactoring" could easily break the system. Let's see: no new features, possible damage, and nothing to show for it at the end. No thank you.

In Part II, we'll talk about how to integrate tidyings into a development workflow. For the moment, read, learn, and apply these tricks that will add joy to your next minutes of development.

CHAPTER 1

Guard Clauses

You see some code like this:

```
if (condition)
    ...some code...
```

Or even better, this:

```
if (condition)
    if (not other condition)
        ...some code...
```

As a reader, it's easy to get lost in nested conditions. Tidy the above to:

```
if (not condition) return
if (other condition) return
...some code...
```

This is easier to read. It says, "Before we get into the details of the code, there are some preconditions we need to bear in mind."

(But what about MuLTipLe ReTuRns? The "rule" about having a single return for a routine came from the days of FORTRAN, where a single routine could have multiple entry *and* exit points. It was nearly impossible to debug such code. You couldn't tell what statements were executed. Code with guard clauses is easier to analyze because the preconditions are explicit.)

Don't overdo guard clauses. A routine with seven or eight guard clauses (I've seen it in the wild) is *not* easier to read. It needs more acute care to partition complexity.

Only tidy to a guard clause if the prompt is met precisely:

```
if (condition)
    ...all the rest of the code in the routine...
```

I see code I want to tidy but can't:

```
if (condition)
    ...some code...
...some other code...
```

Maybe the first two lines can be extracted to a helper method and *then* a guard clause tidied, but *always* and *only* take tiny steps.

Here's an example: *https://github.com/Bogdanp/dramatiq/pull/470.*

CHAPTER 2

Dead Code

Delete it. That's all. If the code doesn't get executed, just delete it.

Deleting dead code can feel mighty strange. After all, someone took the time and effort to write it. The organization paid for it. There it is. All somebody has to do to make it valuable is call it again. If we need it again, we'll be sad we deleted it.

I'll leave it as an exercise for you, tidy reader, to identify all the cognitive biases I just demonstrated.

Sometimes it's easy to identify dead code. Sometimes, because of extensive use of reflection, it's not so easy. If you suspect code isn't used, pre-tidy it by logging its use. Put the pre-tidying into production and wait until you're confident.

You might ask, "But what if we need it later?" That's what version control is for. We aren't really deleting anything. We just don't have to look at it right now. If (and this is a long string of conditionals) we 1) have a lot of code that 2) isn't used right now that 3) we want to use in the future 4) in exactly the same way it was originally written and 5) it still works, then yes, we can get it back. Or we can just write it again, and better. But if worse comes to worst, we can always get it back.

As always, delete only a little code in each tidying diff. That way, if it turns out you were wrong it will be relatively easy to revert the change (see Chapter 28). "A little" is a cognitive measure, not a lines-of-code measure. It could be one clause in a conditional (e.g., you see the condition reduces to true), one routine, one file, one directory.

CHAPTER 3

Normalize Symmetries

Code grows organically. Some folks use "organic" as a pejorative. That makes no sense to me. We can't possibly write all the code we'll ever need all at once. That would only work if we never learned anything.

In growing organically, the same problem may be solved differently at different times or by different people. That's okay, but it makes for difficult reading. As a reader, you'd like consistency. If you see a pattern, you can confidently jump to the conclusion that you know what's going on.

Take the example of lazily initialized variables. You might see them written different ways:

```
foo()
    return foo if foo not nil
    foo := ...
    return foo

foo()
    if foo is nil
        foo := ...
    return foo

# tricky
foo()
    return foo not nil
        ? foo
        : foo := ...

# doubly tricky, assuming assignment is an expression
foo()
    return foo := foo not nil
        ? foo
        : ...
```

```
# even trickier, hiding the conditional
foo()
    return foo := foo || ...
```

(See if you can find or invent more variants.)

All of these are ways of saying, "Compute and cache a value for foo if we haven't already." Each has its pros and cons. You as a reader will quickly get acclimated to any one of them. Things get confusing when two or more of the patterns are used interchangeably. As a reader, you expect that difference means difference. Here you have difference that obscures the fact that the same thing is going on.

Pick a way. Convert one of the variants into that way. Tidy one form of unnecessary variation at a time—lazy initialization, for example, first.

Sometimes the commonality is hidden by extra detail. Look for routines that are similar but not identical. Separate the different parts from the identical parts.

CHAPTER 4

New Interface, Old Implementation

So you need to call a routine, and the interface makes it difficult/complicated/confusing/tedious. Implement the interface you wish you could call and call it. Implement the new interface by simply calling the old one (you can inline the implementation later, after migrating all other callers).

Creating a pass-through interface is the micro-scale essence of software design. You want to make some behavior change. If the design were like thus and so, making that change would be easy(-er). So make the design like that.

The same impulse holds true when you are:

- Coding backward—Start with the last line of a routine, as if you already had all the intermediate results you needed.
- Coding test-first—Start with the test that needs to pass.
- Designing helpers—If only I had a routine/object/service that did *XXX*, then the rest of this would be easy.

CHAPTER 5

Reading Order

Let's say you're reading a file (we can have the debate about whether source code belongs in files some other day). You read the whole file, and you get to the end and there it is! The detail that would have helped you understand all the rest of the file.

Reorder the code in the file in the order in which a reader (remember, there are many readers for each writer) would prefer to encounter it.

You're a reader. You just read it. So you know.

Resist the temptation to apply any other tidyings at the same time. Likely in reading you will have noticed other details that make comprehension and change harder than they should be. There will be time for those details later. Alternatively, tidy those details now and shuffle the reading order in a later tidying. Don't mix.

Some languages are sensitive to the order of declaration of elements. That is, switching the order of declaring function A and function B will produce different execution results. Be careful in such languages. Maybe don't reorder the whole file, just the bits most relevant for readers.

No single ordering of elements is perfect. Sometimes you want to understand the primitives first and then understand how they compose. Sometimes you want to understand the API first and then understand the details of implementation. You're the reader, so use your judgment and (recent) experience. What order would you have liked to encounter? Give the gift of that sequence to the next reader.

CHAPTER 6

Cohesion Order

You read the code, you figure out that to make a behavior change you're going to have to change several widely dispersed spots in the code, and you get grumpy. What should you do?

Reorder the code so the elements you need to change are adjacent. Cohesion order works for routines in a file: if two routines are coupled, put them next to each other. It also works for files in directories: if two files are coupled, put them in the same directory. It even works across repositories: put coupled code in the same repository before changing it.

Why not just eliminate the coupling? If you know how to do that, go for it. That's the best tidying of all, assuming:

$$\text{cost(decoupling)} + \text{cost(change)} < \text{cost(coupling)} + \text{cost(change)}$$

It may not be feasible, though, for various reasons:

- Decoupling can be an intellectual stretch (you don't know how to do it).
- Decoupling can be a time/money stretch (you could do it, but you can't afford to take that time just now).
- Decoupling can be a relationship stretch (the team has taken as much change as it can handle right now).

You aren't stuck with Swiss cheese changes. Tidying can increase cohesion enough to make behavior changes easier. Sometimes the increased clarity from slightly better cohesion unlocks whatever is blocking you from decoupling. Sometimes better cohesion helps you live with the coupling.

CHAPTER 7

Move Declaration and Initialization Together

Variables and their initialization seem to drift apart sometimes. The name of a variable gives you a hint as to its role in the computation. However, the initialization reinforces the message of the name. When you come across code that separates the declaration (with a possible type) and initialization, it's harder to read. By the time you get to the initialization, you've forgotten some of the context of what the variable is *for*.

Here's what this tidying looks like. Imagine you have some code like this:

```
fn()
    int a
    ...some code that doesn't use a
    a = ...
    int b
    ...some more code, maybe it uses a but doesn't use b
    b = ...a...
    ...some code that uses b
```

Tidy this by moving the initialization up to the declaration:

```
fn()
    int a = ...
    ...some code that doesn't use a
    ...some more code, maybe it uses a but doesn't use b
    int b = ...a...
    ...some code that uses b
```

Play around with the order. Is it easier to read and understand the code if each of the variables is declared and initialized just before it's used, or if they're all declared and initialized together at the top of the function? This is where you get to be a mystery writer, imagining the experience of a reader of your code and leaving them the clues they need to guess who done it.

You can't just put variables and code that sets them in any old order. You must respect the data dependencies between variables. If you use a to initialize b, you have to initialize a first. As you're executing this tidying, remember that you have to maintain the order of the data dependencies.

If you have to analyze data dependencies by hand, you are going to eventually make mistakes. You'll accidentally change the behavior of the code when you were just trying to improve its structure. No problem. Back up to a known correct version of the code. Work in smaller steps. That's the tidying way. Big design changes too hard and scary? Take smaller steps. No, smaller. Still scary? No? Good.

CHAPTER 8

Explaining Variables

Some expressions grow. Even if they start small, they grow. And they grow and they grow. And then along you come with your reading glasses on, and you try to understand what's happening.

When you understand a part of a big, hairy expression, extract the subexpression into a variable named after the intention of the expression.

You'll see this frequently in graphics code:

```
return new Point(
    ...big long expression...,
    ...another big long expression...
)
```

Before changing one of those expressions, consider tidying first:

```
x := ...big long expression...
y := ...another big long expression...
return new Point(x, y)
```

Or maybe the expressions mean something more specific, like width and height, top and left, run and rise.

In this tidying you are taking your hard-won understanding and putting it back into the code. This sets you up to change either one of those expressions more easily (because now they are separated), and to read them more quickly next time the code needs to change.

As always, separate the tidying commit from the behavior change commit.

CHAPTER 9

Explaining Constants

So you're reading along, and you see a number you don't recognize. Or you're reading along and you see a constant string repeated all over the code. You figure out what the constant *means*.

Create a symbolic constant. Replace uses of the literal constant with the symbol.

I mean, c'mon. I've been seeing this advice since I was a wee little programmer and yet still somehow folks think this is okay:

```
if response.code = 404
    ...blah blah blah...
```

Okay, I got blame-y there for a second. We're not here to judge the person who made the mess (pro tip: it might be us). We're here to take care of ourselves by tidying first before changing things:

```
PAGE_NOT_FOUND := 404
if response.code = PAGE_NOT_FOUND
    ...blah blah blah...
```

Be careful. The same literal can appear in two places and mean something different. It doesn't help to tidy to:

```
ONE = 1
...ONE... # everywhere you need unity
```

You're reading. You understand. You're putting that understanding into the code so you don't have to hold it in your head.

There are a few tidyings downstream of this one about putting constants that change together or need to be understood together in one place and separating them from constants that cluster for other reasons. I'm going to let you figure those out. Coupling, cohesion, just do your thing.

CHAPTER 10

Explicit Parameters

You're reading some code you want to change, and you notice that some of the data it works on wasn't passed explicitly to the routine. How do you make the inputs clear?

Split the routine. The top part gathers the parameters and passes them explicitly to the second part.

It's common to see blocks of parameters passed in a map. This makes it hard to read and understand what data is required. It also opens up the horrific abuse of modifying the parameters for (implicit) use later.

For example, if you see this:

```
params = { a: 1, b: 2 }
foo(params)

function foo(params)
    ...params.a... ...params.b...
```

Make the parameters explicit by splitting foo:

```
function foo(params)
    foo_body(params.a, params.b)

function foo_body(a, b)
    ...a... ...b...
```

Another case for explicit parameters is when you find the use of environment variables deep in the bowels of the code. Make the parameters explicit, then be prepared to push them up the chain of calling functions. This will make your code easier to read, test, and analyze.

CHAPTER 11

Chunk Statements

This one wins the prize for simplest tidying. You're reading a big chunk of code and you realize, "Oh, this part does *this* and then that part does *that.*" Put a blank line between the parts.

I like that this tidying is so, so simple. That's part of the philosophy of *Tidy First?*—don't make software design such a big deal that you are in danger of not doing it. Software design enables change. A little software design can make change a little easier.

Here's the cool thing—compound interest. Software design also makes more software design easier. This is both a blessing and a curse. You can get caught in the vortex of design and forget to make the change. Don't do that. Done well, software design enables software design that enables change.

After you've chunked statements, you have many paths forward, such as Explaining Variables (Chapter 8), Extract Helper (Chapter 12), or Explaining Comments (Chapter 14).

CHAPTER 12

Extract Helper

You see a block of code inside a routine that has an obvious purpose and limited interaction with the rest of the code in the routine. Extract it as a helper routine. Name the routine after the purpose (not how the routine works).

The refactoring-aware among you will recognize "Extract Method" in this tidying. Executing this tidying/refactoring can be tricky without automated refactoring. That's why you should be in an environment that offers automatic refactoring. It is the 21st century, after all.

I want to mention a couple of special cases of extracting a helper. One is when you have to change a couple of lines within a larger routine. Extract those lines as a helper, change just the lines in the helper, then, if it makes sense, inline the helper back into the calling routine. (Usually you'll find yourself growing fond of the helper and keeping it around.) So, this:

```
routine()
    ...stuff that stays the same...
    ...stuff that needs to change...
    ...stuff that stays the same...
```

becomes:

```
helper()
    ...stuff that needs to change...

routine()
    ...stuff that stays the same...
    helper()
    ...stuff that stays the same...
```

(If you've read ahead you'll recognize this as cohering, or creating a cohesive element. If not, don't worry, we'll get there.)

Another case for extracting a helper is expressing temporal coupling (a( ) needs to be called before b( )). If you see:

```
foo.a()
foo.b()
```

frequently, then create:

```
ab()
    a()
    b()
```

Fondness is not the only reason to keep helpers around. Frequently you'll find yourself wanting to use your new helper again hours or even minutes after you've created it. Interfaces become tools for thinking about problems. New interfaces emerge when we're ready to think more abstractly, to add words to our design vocabulary.

Don't worry about using the helper everywhere it might apply. Using the helper can be taken care of in another tidying. (Some tools will automatically identify and modify all the places where a new helper applies. Heaven bless those tools.)

CHAPTER 13

One Pile

Sometimes you read code that's been split into many tiny pieces, but in a way that hinders you from understanding it. Inline as much of the code as you need until it's all in one big pile. Tidy from there.

The biggest cost of code is the cost of reading and understanding it, not the cost of writing it. Tidy first has a bias toward lots of little pieces, both theoretically, to increase cohesion as a path to reducing coupling, and practically, to reduce the amount of detail that needs to be held in your head at any one time.

The goal of this bias toward small pieces is to enable the code to be understood a little at a time. Sometimes, though, this process goes wrong. Because of how the small pieces interact, the code is *harder* to understand. To regain clarity, the code must first be mooshed together so new, easier-to-understand parts can then be extracted.

Some symptoms you're looking for are:

- Long, repeated argument lists
- Repeated code, especially repeated conditionals
- Poor naming of helper routines
- Shared mutable data structures

Given the bias toward more, smaller pieces, creating one pile feels odd while tidying. However, it's strangely satisfying. I've been trying to understand the code in pieces. I'm starting to doubt my own abilities. I turn 180 degrees and start lumping it all together (it really helps to have automated refactorings for this, but I'll do it manually if I have to). What a relief!

As the pile gets bigger, the shape starts to emerge in my mind. I see—first we calculate this, then we use it to calculate that! Why didn't they just say so? Now I get to ask the title question: should I tidy first? Or just make the change I can now see?

CHAPTER 14

Explaining Comments

You know that moment when you're reading some code and you say, "Oh, so *that's* what's going on!" That's a valuable moment. Record it.

Write down only what wasn't obvious from the code. Put yourself in the place of the future reader, or yourself 15 minutes ago. What is it that you would have liked to have known? You might make a note like, "The following is complicated by the need to reduce the number of network calls as much as possible."

Write to someone specific, even if they aren't much like you. Are you the only biologist on your team of computer scientists? Then you'd better explain any biology context in the code, even if it seems obvious to you. The point is to think from the perspective of someone else, and try to preemptively address likely questions.

If you encounter a file with no header comment, consider adding a header telling prospective readers why they might find reading this file useful. (Thanks, Allan Mertner.)

Immediately upon finding a defect is a good time to comment. For example, `// Be sure to change ../foo if you add another case`. It's not ideal to have that coupling in your code. Eventually, you'll have to learn how to eliminate it, but in the meantime, it's much better to add the comment that points out the coupling issue, rather than leaving it buried in the sand.

CHAPTER 15

Delete Redundant Comments

When you see a comment that says exactly what the code says, remove it.

The purpose of code is to explain to other programmers what you want the computer to do. Comments and code present different trade-offs for you as a writer and for future readers. You can explain anything you want in prose. On the other hand, there's no mechanism to double-check the accuracy of prose as the system changes, and comments might become redundant as the code evolves.

Some folks take a narrow view of the mandate to communicate, insisting on dogmatic rules like one stating that every routine must be commented. This results in comments like:

```
getX()
  # return X
  return X
```

This comment provides costs without benefits. As a writer, you've just wasted the reader's time—time they can't recover. If a comment is completely redundant, then delete it.

Tidyings often chain together. A previous tidying may have made a comment redundant. For example, the original code might look like this:

```
if (generator)
    ...a bunch of lines of code to set up the generator...
else
    # no generator, return the default
    return getDefaultGenerator()
```

After tidying with a guard clause, the code looks like this:

```
if (! generator)
    # no generator, return the default
    return getDefaultGenerator()
```

```
...a bunch of lines of code to set up the generator...
```

The comment isn't redundant at first. It returns our attention to the current context (no generator present) after reading a bunch of lines of code in a different context (generator present, needs setup). After tidying, however, the comment is a simple restatement of what the code says. So, let's delete it. *Hasta la vista, auf wiedersehen,* buh-bye.

We'll talk more about chaining tidyings in Part II.

Managing

Tidying is software design addressing you, your relationship to your code, and ultimately your relationship with yourself. In the next book in the series, we'll talk about how and why teams perform software design together. After that we'll talk about software design and its role in relationships with nonprogrammers. Tidying is geek self-care.

The mechanics of the tidyings will come to you with practice. Most of them require no automated support. Programming environments inexplicably lack automated support for refactoring even now, decades after it became feasible. But okay. I want you to get used to designing software a little at a time, all the time. Tidyings are gateway refactorings.

Just being able to identify that a tidying applies and applying it doesn't mean you've mastered tidying. The title of this book is *Tidy First?*, with emphasis on the question mark. I wanted to acknowledge that just because you can tidy doesn't mean you should tidy.

This section on managing tidying discusses how to fit tidying into a personal development workflow:

- When do you start tidying?
- When do you stop tidying?
- How do you combine tidying, changing the structure of the code, with changing the behavior of the system?

We'll start by discussing how tidying interacts with pull requests and code reviews.

CHAPTER 16

Separate Tidying

We'll assume for the moment that you use a pull request (PR)/code review model (I'll argue for an alternative later). Where do you put tidyings?

Here's an ugly piece of tail chasing:

1. I put my tidyings in with my behavior changes.
2. Reviewers complain that my PRs are too long.
3. I separate the tidyings into their own PRs, either before (more likely) or after the behavior changes.
4. Reviewers complain that the tidying PRs are pointless.
5. Go to 1.

The tidyings have to go somewhere, or you don't tidy. Where do they go? Summary: they go in their own PRs, with as few tidyings per PR as possible.

Let's go through the trade-offs in more depth. Folks learning to tidy seem to go through predictable phases. In the first phase we're just making changes, and we begin with an undifferentiated mass of changes (Figure 16-1).

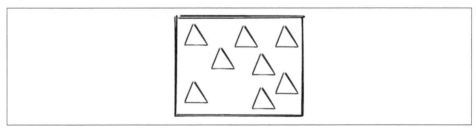

Figure 16-1. Undifferentiated mass of changes

Here, we're in the middle of fixing an `if` statement, realize a name is wrong, fix that, and go back to the `if` statement. Change is change.

After learning the tidyings, it's as if our picture under the microscope snaps into focus. Some of those changes were changing the behavior of the program, its attributes as observed from the running of the program. Some of those changes, though, were changing the structure of the program. Those changes can only be observed by looking at the code: B=behavior, S=structure (Figure 16-2).

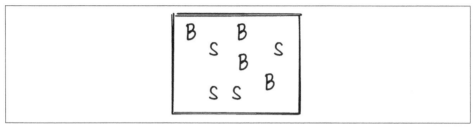

Figure 16-2. Behavior changes and structure changes

At this point there is still no plan, and no flow between changing behavior and structure—just an awareness that there are two different things playing together.

After a bit of this, we start noticing the common flows. Chunking statements leads to explaining helpers leads to an easier time making behavior changes. Now programming is more like chess, and you can guess how the game will play out several moves (or sequences) ahead (Figure 16-3).

Figure 16-3. Behavior and structure changes in sequence

Note that we still have one big PR at this point. We're at step 1 of the loop. Every move we made was intentional, aimed either at making easy changes or making those changes easy. Put it all together, though, and it's a bit of a mess. Reviewers will balk.

And so we split our changes into separate PRs. Sequences of tidyings (or even just one tidying) go in one PR. Behavior changes go in a separate PR. Each time we switch between tidying and changing behavior, we open a new PR (Figure 16-4).

Figure 16-4. Behavior and structure changes in separate PRs

How you lump or split your PRs is a trade-off. Think of it in terms of incentives. A big, all-inclusive PR shows a whole picture but may be too much for a reviewer to provide useful feedback on. Teensy-tiny PRs invite feedback in the small sense, but it comes at the risk of going off into the weeds.

Review latency is also an incentive. If code gets reviewed rapidly, then you're encouraged to create more, smaller PRs. Those more-focused PRs encourage even more rapid reviews. Equally, this reinforcing loop can run backward, with slow reviews encouraging larger PRs, further slowing future reviews.

Once you get comfortable with tidying, with working in small steps, with working with absolute safety, I encourage you to experiment with not requiring reviews for tidying PRs. This reduces latency further, incentivizing even smaller tidying PRs.

CHAPTER 17

Chaining

Tidyings are like potato chips. You eat one, and you'll want another. Managing the urge to keep tidying is a key tidying skill. You just tidied; should you tidy more? It depends (we'll get to what it depends on in Part III).

How big you step will be up to you, but I encourage you to experiment with sticking to tiny tidying steps. Optimize each step. From the outside it will look like you are running, but, like the centipede, you will know you're taking many little steps.

Tidying becomes a game of chess, with moves visible ahead. Let's look at how tidyings set up further tidyings:

Guard clause
> Once you've set up a guard clause, the condition may benefit from being turned into an explaining helper or extracted into an explaining variable.

Dead code
> Once you've removed the clutter of dead code, you may be able to see how to sort the code into reading order or cohesion order.

Normalize symmetries
> Once you've made identical code identical and different code different, you may be able to group precisely parallel code into reading order. I did this once with a file containing several web entry points. Once they all looked alike, it was natural to group them at the top of the file as a kind of table of contents to the rest of the code.

New interface, old implementation
> Once you have your shiny new interface, you'll want to use it. If you don't have the automated rewrite tools to convert all callers, you'll need to convert them one at a time. This is the first time we've seen fanout—when one tidying leads to a

bunch more, each of which can lead to a bunch more (way more about this when we talk about coupling and power laws).

Reading order

After you've established reading order, you may see the opportunity to normalize symmetries. Before, elements were far enough apart that you couldn't see the similarities.

Cohesion order

Elements grouped together for cohesion order are candidates to be extracted into a subelement. Creating, for example, a helper object is out of the scope of tidying. As you get comfortable and confident in tidying, though, it's natural to see larger-scale design changes that will ease further behavior changes.

Explaining variables

The righthand side of the assignment to an explaining variable is a candidate for an explaining helper (after which you may be able to inline the variable). The explanation offered by the variable name may make it possible to delete redundant comments.

Explaining constants

Extracting an explaining constant leads to cohesion order. Grouping constants that change in sync eases future changes.

There are whole philosophies about where to put constants and how to arrange them. I won't get into all that here—pick something that makes your work easy. Well, easier.

Explicit parameters

After making parameters explicit, you may be able to group a set of parameters into an object and move code into that object. This is out of the scope of tidying, but be on the lookout for new abstractions revealed as you tidy. Some of the most powerful abstractions you will ever discover derive from running code. You would never have created them on speculation.

Chunk statements

You can precede each chunk with an explaining comment. You may extract a chunk as an explaining helper.

Extract helper

After extracting a helper you may introduce a guard clause, extract explaining constants and variables, or delete redundant comments.

One pile

After making a big, obvious mess, expect to tidy by chunking statements, adding explaining comments, and extracting helpers.

Explaining comments

Move the information in the comment into the code if possible, by introducing an explaining variable, explaining constant, or explaining helper.

Delete redundant comments

Eliminating the noise of redundant comments can help you see a better reading order or see the chance for explicit parameters.

I'm going to emphasize once again, since I get accused of being anti-comment, that you should only delete absolutely, completely redundant comments. You should also tidy with an eye toward making comments absolutely, completely redundant. Your job as a software designer is to set yourself and your team up for success, now and in the future.

Since change is the dominant cost of software development and understanding code is the dominant cost of change, communicating the structure and intent of working code is one of the most valuable skills you can exercise. Comments are *a* form of communication, but tidying lets you explore the limits of communicating through the other elements of programming.

Conclusion

You will begin to flow tidyings together to achieve larger changes to the structure of your code. Be wary of changing too much, too fast. A failed tidying is expensive relative to the cost of a series of successful tidyings. Practice tidyings like the notes of a scale. When the notes are clean and relaxed, you can form them into melodies.

Batch Sizes

How much tidying should you do before integrating and deploying?

Well, there are a couple of considerations:

- How much tidying do you need to do? That is, if we define "tidying" as structural changes supporting the next behavior change, then how many structural changes do you need to make to support the next behavior change? Tidying is not looking toward a far-ahead future. Tidying meets an immediate need. (We'll talk about this more when we talk about first/after/later, in Chapter 21.)

- How much tidying will be easy to integrate and deploy?

In Chapter 16, I discussed not mixing tidying and behavior changes. But we still have the open question of whether we batch all our tidyings together, do them all separately, or something in between (Figure 18-1).

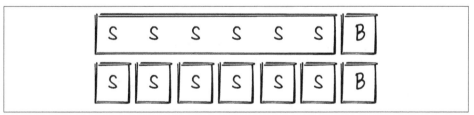

Figure 18-1. Structure changes batched together or separately

This puts us in a trade-off space, also known as a Goldilocks dilemma. What are the competing costs that let us evaluate what constitutes too few tidyings per batch, too many tidyings per batch, and the range of just the right number of tidyings per batch (Figure 18-2)?

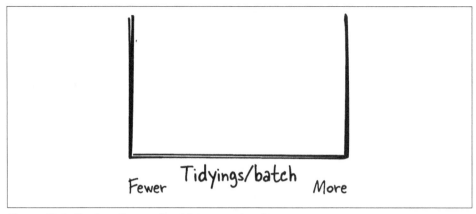

Figure 18-2. Trade-off space for tidyings per batch

Figure 18-3 shows the costs that rise as we put more tidyings in a batch.

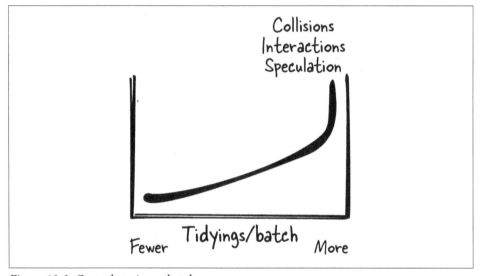

Figure 18-3. Costs that rise as batches grow

These include:

Collisions

The more tidyings per batch, the longer the delay before integrating, and the greater the chance that a tidying collides with work someone else is doing. As soon as we encounter a merge conflict, the cost of merging our work rises by an order of magnitude. (Please remember that all these "numbers" are only directionally accurate, meant to help train your intuition.)

Interactions

Likewise, the chance of a batch accidentally changing behavior rises with the number of tidyings in the batch. And likewise, merge costs rise dramatically when we have an interaction.

Speculation

I know we said we were only going to tidy just enough to support the next behavior change, but yeah. The more tidyings per batch, the more we are prone to tidying just because, with all the additional costs that creates.

All of these factors reduce the number of tidyings we want in a batch before integrating and deploying (which are the same thing, right?). Yet, I see big batches of tidyings in the wild. What else is going on? Take a look at Figure 18-4.

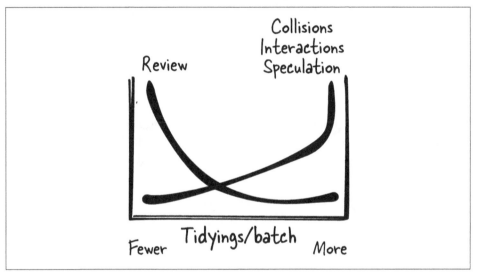

Figure 18-4. Review costs rise as batches shrink

In many organizations, the fixed cost of getting a single change through review and deployment is substantial. Programmers feel this cost, so they move right in the trade-off space, even as the costs of collisions, interactions, and speculation rise.

What to do, what to do?

Some folks act like these cost curves are inscribed on stone tablets, laws of the physics of the development universe we merely inhabit. Nope. If we want to reduce the cost of tidying, thus increasing tidying and reducing the cost of making behavior changes, then we can reduce the cost of review (Figure 18-5).

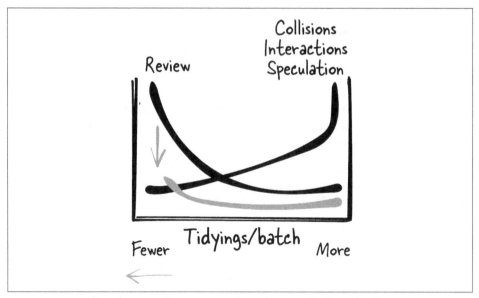

Figure 18-5. Reduce the cost of review to reduce the cost of tidying by shrinking batches

You and your team are going to need to figure out how exactly to reduce the cost of review. In teams with trust and a strong culture, tidyings don't require review. The risk of interactions has been reduced so far that unreviewed tidying doesn't destabilize the software.

Getting to the necessary level of safety and trust to eliminate tidying reviews is the work of months. Practice. Experiment. Review errors together.

CHAPTER 19

Rhythm

Let's go back to the beginning. You are tidying to make future changes to the behavior of the system easier. You are making future behavior changes easier because you're worth it (we'll get into the economics later, if anyone objects). What are we talking about here? A brief moment, then back to the slog? Hour upon hour of blissful tidying?

Part of the art of managing tidying is managing the rhythm of it. In the previous chapter, we saw this image (Figure 19-1), encouraging smaller batches of tidying.

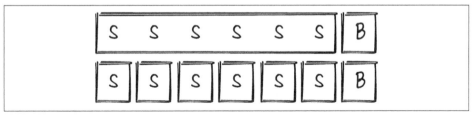

Figure 19-1. Structure changes batched together or separately

How much time is represented in one of those successions of structure changes followed by a behavior change?

Well, software design is fractal, so it could be any time scale. For the purposes of this book, however, we are talking about one scale of software design: software design with personal impact. For that, we are talking about minutes, up to an hour. More than an hour of tidying at a time before making a behavior change likely means you've lost track of the minimum set of structure changes needed to enable your desired behavior change.

Another possibility, though, is that the code is in such a mess that you can profitably tidy for hours before making a behavior change. If this is true, it won't be true for long. Software design has a strong "pave the path" tendency.

If you haven't heard the story, here's how it goes: a college built a bunch of buildings, and the planners were trying to figure out where to put walking paths between them. Rather than make carefully educated guesses, however, they just planted all the area between the buildings with grass.

A few months later, students' feet had worn paths in the grass. The planners paved those areas that had been worn smooth.

Behavior changes tend to cluster in the code. From Pareto, 80% of the changes will occur in 20% of the files. One of the beauties of tidying first is that the tidyings cluster too. And they cluster in exactly those spots most attractive for behavior changes.

Even if at first you tidy a *lot*, soon you will find yourself wanting to make a behavior change in code that's already tidy. Continue for a bit, and most changes will happen in already-tidied areas of the code. Eventually, encountering untidy code will be the exception, even though most of the code in the system hasn't been touched.

That's why I'm confident in saying that tidying is a minutes-to-an-hour kind of activity. Yes, sometimes it goes on longer, but not for long.

CHAPTER 20

Getting Untangled

You're changing the behavior of some code. You see a tidying that would make it easier to change. You tidy. Then you write another test case. Now you need to change the behavior some more. That leads to more tidying. An hour later you:

- Actually understand all the behavior changes that need to be made
- Actually understand all the tidying that eases those behavior changes
- Have a mess of tidyings and changes all tangled together

You have at least three options, none of them attractive:

- Ship it as is. This is impolite to reviewers and prone to errors, but it's quick.
- Untangle the tidyings and changes into separate PRs, or a sequence of PRs, or a sequence of commits in a single PR. This is more polite, but it can be a lot of work.
- Discard your work in progress and start over, tidying first. This is more work, but it leaves a coherent chain of commits.

The sunk cost fallacy complicates the choice between these options. You have some new tests. They pass. Why would you want to throw that away?

The answer, as always, is because you are not just instructing a computer, you are explaining your intentions for the computer to other people. The shortest path to instructing the computer is not an interesting end goal.

By this point in the book it may not surprise you that I encourage you to experiment with the last option. Re-implementation raises the possibility that you will see something new as you re-implement, letting you squeeze more value out of the same set of behavior changes.

Untangling a ball of yarn starts with noticing that you have a tangle. The sooner you realize the need to untangle, the smaller the job is (and the less important the decision between the strategies becomes). When you first begin consciously tidying, whether first or after, you'll likely miss the transition between "cruising along making changes" and "oh no, what all have I done?" Don't worry. You'll get better at sequencing tidyings and changes over time.

Speaking of "first or after," it's time to talk about timing.

CHAPTER 21

First, After, Later, Never

Let's talk about the timing of tidying with respect to a behavior change in the system. Tidy first, then change the behavior? Change the behavior, then tidy? Or simply note messiness (in the sense that future behavior changes are going to be harder than they need to be), then come back later to tidy? Or, don't tidy at all?

Never

Let's start with the last one. As always, we need to examine the trade-offs involved in not tidying at all. When should we say, "Yes, this is a giant mess, and we consciously choose not to do anything about it"? The best reason is because we're never going to change the behavior of the code ever, ever again.

I stated the condition like that because it's rare that code truly never needs to have its behavior changed. However, it does happen. For truly static systems, "If it ain't broke, don't fix it" reasonably applies.

Later

Some folks think tidying later is pure fantasy, a unicorn, an honest politician. The mythological status of tidying later is used as justification for tidying too much now, whether that is before or after. I'm here to tell you that you really *can* tidy later. You may not like the prerequisite, though.

Is there enough time to do your work? I'm not asking whether you have *plenty* of time, because of course not. I'm not asking whether there's more to do than you have time for, because of course there is. Ask yourself, "How would we work if we had enough time?" If the answer is wildly different from what you are actually doing, then no, there is not enough time to do your work.

But I invite you to examine this assumption that there isn't enough time to do your work. I've worked with large, successful, long-lived, highly profitable businesses that still believed, in the face of all the evidence of being large, successful, long-lived, and highly profitable, that there just wasn't and wouldn't ever be enough time to do the work. Seems bizarre, like a bird questioning the laws of physics and suddenly falling out of the sky.

What would you do if you temporarily, provisionally believed that there was enough time to do your work? You might make a list of messes to tidy later (I call this my Fun List, because I have an odd notion of "fun"). Then later, rather than jumping feverishly to the next feature to implement, you might glance at your Fun List and think, "I have an hour. I don't want to start something big. Why don't I take a crack at item 4?" And then you might.

That's tidying later. It can happen. Try it. Then it *will* happen.

Tidying makes future changes to the behavior of the system easier (through mechanisms we will explore in the next part of the book). If there is an area of the system that's guaranteed to change (strong word, "guaranteed"), then tidying in that general area creates value if it simplifies those future changes.

Tidying later (that is, not tied to an immediate behavior change) creates value in a couple of other ways. One is by reducing the tax of messiness. You are migrating from an old API to a new API. You've changed the call sites that are immediately affected, but you have one hundred more call sites to migrate later. When you've migrated them all, you can remove the old API. However, until then, you have to mirror changes made to the new API in the old API.

Tidying all those call sites isn't pointless mucking about. Once you migrate all of the changes, a certain class of changes becomes cheaper. There may not be a pressing need to reduce that cost, but taking the pebble out of your shoe lets you walk better.

Another reason to tidy later is as a learning tool. The code "knows" how it wants to be structured. If you're listening and you move the code from its current structure toward its desired structure, you're bound to learn something. Tidying is a great way to become aware of the detailed consequences of your design. Tidying illuminates the design as it could be.

Finally, tidying later just feels good. Software development is a human process. We are humans with human needs. Sometimes I just don't have the energy to tackle a new feature, but I want to work. Picking an item off the Fun List and tidying it brings me joy. Don't underestimate how much better you are as a programmer when you're happy.

After

You need to change behavior. The code is messy. You can't see how to tidy. You change the behavior anyway (good for you—mess is no excuse). But now, huzzah!, you see how the change you made could have been easier. Do you tidy after?

It depends. Are you ever going to change the behavior in this same area again? (Likely yes, for reasons we'll get into in the next section, but still apply your judgment.) If you're going to change the area again, then a tidy after approach makes some sense.

Why not just tidy first the next time you need to change behavior in this area? It might be harder later. You may have forgotten context that makes tidying easier right now. Other changes may have interfered with the tidying you'd like to do now. If waiting to tidy at a later date substantially increases the cost of tidying, consider doing it now.

Also, how much tidying are we talking about? Say the behavior change took you an hour. Spending an hour tidying after makes sense. Spending a week tidying after? That doesn't make sense. That goes on the Fun List.

So sure, tidy after, if:

- You're going to change the same area again. Soon.
- It's cheaper to tidy now.
- The cost of tidying is roughly in proportion to the cost of behavior changes.

First

Now here, finally, at the end of the second part of the book, we come to an answer to the question posed by its title. Tidy first? And the answer is…

It depends.

I love my job sometimes. So okay, yeah, of course it depends, but what does it depend on? I need to change the behavior of this code. This code is messy. Do I tidy first? Ask yourself these questions:

- How much harder is the messy change? If tidying doesn't make it any easier, don't tidy first.
- How immediate is the benefit of tidying? Let's say you're not ready to change the behavior yet. You're just reading code for comprehension. Tidying helps you comprehend faster. Sure, tidy first.

- How will this tidying amortize? If you'll only ever change this code once, then consider limiting your tidying. If this tidying will pay off weekly for years, then go for it.

- How sure are you of your tidying? Bias away from speculation. "I can see the messiness here, right here. If it's gone, then this change will be easy." But also, "Tidying this will make it easier to understand. I know because I'm confused right now."

In general, bias toward tidying first, but be wary of tidying becoming an end in itself. The tidyings I've cataloged are tiny precisely so you don't have to think too hard about applying them. If you tidy and it doesn't pay off, no big deal. Bias toward tidying shouldn't cost you much, and most of the time it will pay off.

Summary

Tidy never when:

- You're never changing this code again.
- There's nothing to learn by improving the design.

Tidy later when:

- You have a big batch of tidying to do without immediate payoff.
- There's eventual payoff for completing the tidying.
- You can tidy in little batches.

Tidy after when:

- Waiting until next time to tidy first will be more expensive.
- You won't feel a sense of completion if you don't tidy after.

Tidy first when:

- It will pay off immediately, either in improved comprehension or in cheaper behavior changes.
- You know what to tidy and how.

PART III

Theory

Now that we've seen *what* to tidy and *how* and *when* to tidy, we can discuss *why* to tidy. You don't need to know exactly how a medication works to experience its effects, but knowing how it works gives you a deeper appreciation of it and allows you to use the medication in novel circumstances.

Theory doesn't convince. No one is going to say, "Tidying is bullshit. Oh, wait, you're creating optionality. I guess it's a good idea after all."

Understanding theory optimizes application. The forever questions in software design are:

- When do I start making software design decisions?
- When do I stop making software design decisions and get on with changing the behavior of the system?
- How do I make the next decision?

These questions aren't rationally, logically answerable because the information needed to find rational, logical answers doesn't exist when we ask the questions.

Understanding theory sharpens your judgment for when you have to answer these questions on speculation. Understanding theory lets you disagree constructively with your fellow geeks.

Sometimes when I want to do X and you want to do Y, what we disagree about is simple. We are both trying to accomplish the same goal but in different ways. Theory helps when our disagreement runs deeper. When we are trying to accomplish different goals, this is when sharing a theoretical framework becomes valuable.

If we disagree in principle and we can discuss our principles, then we have a chance to agree on what to do sooner. We also have a chance to learn from each other. When we're stuck on "X," "No, Y," then we're stuck in a battle of wills, likely to be resolved through our relative power positions in our relationship.

This part of the book addresses the following questions:

1. What *is* software design?
2. How does software design drive the cost of software development and operation, and how does the cost of software development and operation drive software design?
3. What are the trade-offs between investing in the structure of software and not investing in the structure of software?
4. What principles, economic and human, can we use to inform whether and how to change the structure of software?

We started this whole journey by saying that "software design is an exercise in human relationships." This book is primarily focused on your relationship with yourself: do you value yourself enough to make your work easier before you do the work? But this is only step one in the journey. In this section, we'll consider one of the most persistent, complicated aspects of human relationships: money.

CHAPTER 22

Beneficially Relating Elements

What is software design? I'm not a fan of starting with definitions, but we're hardly starting by now. You've seen examples of what I mean by design. You've seen how individual decisions chain together to achieve larger goals. You've seen the first glimpses of what I mean by "software design is an exercise in human relationships." Now I can say what I mean by "software design": *beneficially relating elements*.

That's not many words for a big concept. Each word must be carrying substantial weight. Let's pick them apart and then put them back together.

Elements

Substantial structures have parts.

Organelle → organ → organism.

Atoms → molecules → crystals.

In our world: tokens → expressions → statements → functions → objects/modules → systems.

Elements have boundaries. You know where they start and end.

Elements contain subelements. In our world we like to have homogeneous hierarchies (*à la* Composite pattern). Natural hierarchies, like previous examples, are not homogeneous. Contained subelements differ from the container. (I'm not sure this point is terribly important, but I like to keep it in mind—someday I'll write a truly philosophical book about software design as a natural process.)

Relating

Okay, so we have a hierarchy of elements. Those elements exist in relation to each other. One function calls another. The functions are the elements. "Calls/called by" is the relationship. In the natural world, we have relationships like "eats," "shades," and "fertilizes."

In software design, we have a handful of relationships like:

- Invokes
- Publishes
- Listens
- Refers (as in fetching the value of a variable)

Beneficially

Here's where the magic happens. One design is to have a single gigantic soup of tiny subelements. Think assembly language with a global namespace. This program would work. It would behave from the point of view of an external observer exactly the same as a well-designed program. Quickly, however, we would be unable to change it. There would be too many relationships, often implicit, between the elements.

When we design, creating intermediate elements between the machine instructions and the whole, those intermediate elements begin benefitting each other. Function A can be simpler because function B takes care of the complexity of a part of the calculation.

Beneficially Relating Elements

One reading of the phrase "beneficially relating elements" starts with "the design is…." What is the design? It's the elements, their relationships, and the benefits derived from those relationships.

Another reading starts with "designers are…." What do designers do? They beneficially relate elements. From this perspective, software designers can only:

- Create and delete elements.
- Create and delete relationships.
- Increase the benefit of a relationship.

There—easy, right? (← sarcasm warning)

Take one of my favorite examples. I have an object that invokes another object twice in one function:

```
caller()
    return box.width() * box.height()
```

The calling function has two relationships with the box, those of invoking two functions. Let's move the expression into the box:

```
caller()
    return box.area()

Box>>area()
    return width() * height()
```

From a design standpoint, we have created a new element, `Box.area()`, and adjusted the relationship between the caller and the box. Now they are related by a single function invocation, with the benefit that the calling function is simpler and the cost that `Box` is one function bigger.

When I talk about the structure of the system, I'm talking about:

- The element hierarchy
- The relationships between elements
- The benefits created by those relationships

Now we can make a firmer distinction between the structure and the behavior of the system.

CHAPTER 23

Structure and Behavior

Software creates value in two ways:

- What it does today
- The possibility of new things we can make it do tomorrow

"What it does today" is the system's behavior—calculating payroll, sending dropship orders, notifying friends. (And yes, all software systems are sociotechnical systems, and we won't be designing the socio- part of it just yet.)

Behavior can be characterized in two ways:

Input/output pairs
 This many hours at this pay rate in this jurisdiction should result in a paycheck like this and a tax filing like that.

Invariants
 The sum of all entitlements should equal the sum of all deductions.

Behavior creates value. Rather than having to calculate a bunch of numbers by hand, the computer can calculate millions of them every second. Turns out people will pay not to have to calculate numbers by hand. If running the software costs $1 in electricity and you can charge folks $10 to run it on their behalf, then you have a business.

In theory, this business could run forever, producing $10 for every dollar we put in. We know this is an oversimplification. Bit rot is real. Something is always changing. Staying in place in the river requires constant paddling. But for purposes of the distinction I'm drawing, this is good enough for the moment.

You know what's better than a machine that spits out $10 for every $1 you put in? A machine that spits out $100 for every $10 you put in. Or $20 for every $1. How are we going to get to that better machine?

In a word, optionality. The mere presence of a system behaving a certain way changes the desire for how the system should behave (Heisenberg's uncertainty principle). However much you'd pay for the $10/$1 machine, you'd pay more for one that could turn into either a $100/$10 machine or a $20/$1 machine—*even if you didn't know which it would turn into.*

This is the secret it took me decades to absorb. I didn't have to change the behavior of my system to make it more valuable. As soon as I added to the options of what it *could* do next, I had already made money. (I went down the rabbit hole of options pricing formulas to really cement this understanding, but I trust you to figure out how to convince yourself.)

Options are the economic magic of software—especially the option to expand. If you can build 1,000 cars, there's no guarantee you can build 100,000 cars. But if you can send 1,000 notifications, you almost certainly can, with work, send 100,000 (when we get to the outer limits of technology, expansion becomes less certain, but in early growth, expansion isn't risky).

One of the coolest thing about options is that the more volatile the environment is, the more valuable options become. This was part of my motivation to subtitle my book *Extreme Programming Explained* "Embrace Change." As a young engineer, I was terrified when a seemingly settled situation turned chaotic. As I learned to enhance optionality, I saw chaos as an opportunity.

What interferes with options? Here are some scenarios that reduce the options value embedded in your software:

- A key employee quits. Changes that would have taken days now take months.
- You distance yourself from your customers. If you get a provocative suggestion a month instead of one every day, you have fewer options.
- The cost of changes skyrockets. Instead of being able to exercise an option a day, you can only exercise an option a month. Fewer options, less value.

Nothing in the scope of this book directly addresses the first two of these options killers, but we can react to the third. We can keep the kitchen clean as we cook.

The structure of the system doesn't matter to its behavior. One big function, a whole bunch of itty bitties, same paycheck comes out. The structure creates options. The structure could make it easy to add new countries to our paycheck calculation, or it could make it hard.

Here's the problem: structure is not legible in the same way behavior is legible. There's a reason product roadmaps are lists of features (behavior changes). It's easy to see when the behavior changes—a button appears that wasn't there before.

Even though we know that we have to invest in structure to maintain and expand optionality, we can't really tell if we have. The code is easier to change? Really? We can't really tell if we've done enough. If we invested more in the structure, the code would be even easier to change? Really? We can't really tell if we've made the right investments in structure. The structure changes we made were the best way to make the code easier to change? Really?

And so people get muddled about structure changes in ways they don't about behavior changes. This book is not here to answer those questions for you; it's here to help you answer those questions for yourself. Start by understanding that structure changes and behavior changes are both ways to create value, but that they are fundamentally different. How? In a word, reversibility.

CHAPTER 24

Economics: Time Value and Optionality

Somehow I got to my mid-30s understanding nothing about the nature of money. I could buy and sell stuff, I could "make" money, but I didn't understand the physics of moving money at all.

Computing came to the rescue. A series of finance-related projects forced me to program basic money-related concepts. Since programming is how I understand the world, I started to understand money. Over time the lessons soaked into my intuition and changed how I saw development.

James Buchan in *Frozen Desire* (Picador) makes the case that we often want stuff but not right away, and that money represents this "frozen desire." If you have created enough value to eat for a month, but you don't want to store a month's food, it's extremely convenient to be able to store the value you've created and turn it into fresh lettuce a week at a time.

Money, though, is curious stuff. It has its own nature. The combination of money's nature and money's centrality to the work we do leads to tension. What makes sense for us to do as programmers may go contrary to the nature of money. When geeky imperatives clash with money imperatives, money wins. Eventually.

Once my lessons in the nature of money had soaked into my intuition, I found my attitude toward programming shifting. Strategies that had made perfect sense to me now seemed bizarre where they contradicted the nature of money. Strategies that had seemed fringe or sketchy or naive became just sensible money management. The more I rowed with the Stream of Commerce, the faster my boat went.

The nature I learned consisted of two surprising properties:

- A dollar today is worth more than a dollar tomorrow, so earn sooner and spend later.
- In a chaotic situation, options are better than things, so create options in the face of uncertainty.

These two strategies conflict at times. Earning money now can reduce future options. But maybe if you don't earn money now, you won't be around to exercise those future options.

If you already understand NPV and options greeks, feel free to skip the next two chapters. If, like to the me of 30 years ago, "NPV and options greeks" sounds like gibberish to you, then carry on to learn a bit about these first two phrases in the financial phrasebook. Just as it feels good to be able to say, "Where's the bathroom?" and "Another beer, please," in a new country, the following two chapters will help you begin to navigate FinanceWorld and finance's profound influence on software design.

Software design has to reconcile the imperatives of "earn sooner/spend later" and "create options, not things." We'll get to how software design interacts with money after we've looked at these two effects—the time value of money and optionality—in more detail.

CHAPTER 25

A Dollar Today > A Dollar Tomorrow

More is more and less is less, right? Depends. With money, it depends on:

- When
- How sure

If I give you a dollar today, you can spend it on something you want or you can invest it in a way that gives you more money later. If I promise you a dollar tomorrow, it's worth less than the dollar I give you today. Why?

- You can't spend it, so it's worth less.
- You can't invest it, so when you get it, it will be worth less than the dollar you got today.
- There's some chance that I won't actually give it to you. Well, not me. I'm entirely trustworthy. But someone else, yeah, you have to be prepared that they won't give you the dollar, making that "dollar tomorrow" worth less.

How much less? This is a complicated question. For now, the important fact is that all dollars are not valued equally. If we want to, for example, add them up, then we need a date attached to each one.

How do we value a software system? Say you have a software system and I want to buy it. How much should I reasonably pay you?

What it *is* is irrelevant. It's a payment system. It consists of umpteen services. It has 1.4 million lines of code. Its average function cyclomatic complexity is 14 (just kidding, the average of power law–distributed values is useless). But none of this matters to me as a purchaser.

As a purchaser, I want to know how the money is going to flow. "Gazinttas and gaz-outtas," as my Pappy would have said. To value the software, I can model it as a set of cash flows, some in, some out, but (and this is the key point) each flow connected to a date.

Here's an exercise to help sharpen your intuition about time/money. Which is more attractive, a software system that over the next 10 years will cost $10 million and bring in $20 million, or one that will cost $10 million and bring in $12 million?

It's a trick question. "Over the next 10 years" is financially equivalent to saying, "Until the heat death of the universe." The intuition to sharpen is, when you see those numbers, to immediately ask, "Yeah, but when and how sure?"

Feel the difference between "I pay $10 million today and in 10 years I get $20 million" and "I get $12 million today and in 10 years I pay $10 million." That first deal makes me nervous. Yes, it seems like a good investment, but I'm going to be sweating out those 10 years. The second deal is a no-brainer. I'm guaranteed $2 million profit from day 1, plus whatever I get from investing over the 10 years. I'm excited about the 10 years instead of afraid of it.

In the scope of this book, the time value of money encourages tidy after over tidy first. If we can implement a behavior change that makes us money now and tidy after, we make money sooner and spend money later. (As noted earlier, sometimes tidying first means the total cost of tidying first + behavior change is less than the cost of the behavior change without tidying. Always tidy first in such a case.)

At the scale we are talking about, minutes to hours, discounting cash flows probably doesn't make a huge economic difference. It does make a difference, though. Practicing with time value will help us in later books as we move to larger scales.

Next we'll look at the other source of software's economic value: optionality. Fun times, because time value and option value often conflict.

CHAPTER 26

Options

The previous chapter modeled the economic value of a software system as the sum of the discounted future cash flows. We create value when we change those flows:

- Earning money more, sooner, and with greater likelihood
- Spending money less, later, and with less likelihood

Working inside this model as a software designer already isn't easy. We live in a Goldilocks world: not too much design or too soon, not too little design or too late. But wait, there's more. (If it was easy, everybody would already be doing it and there'd be no excuse for this book.) There's another, sometimes conflicting, source of value: optionality.

Decades back I worked with trading software on Wall Street. I did the background reading, as I like to do, and discovered options pricing. Down the rabbit hole I went. I had recently invented test-driven development (TDD), and I was looking for practice topics. Options pricing seemed like a great example: complicated algorithm with known answers.

I implemented the extant options pricing formulas test first (discovering the need for an epsilon when comparing floating-point numbers in the process). Along the way I developed an intuition for options that started to leak out into my general thinking about software design.

I can't implement all those algorithms for you, but I can report the lessons I learned (I encourage you to try the exercise if you really want to "get it"):

- "What behavior can I implement next?" has value all on its own, even before I implement it. This surprised me. I thought I was getting paid for what I had done (as per the previous chapter). I wasn't. I was mostly getting paid for what I could do next.
- "What behavior can I implement next?" is more valuable the more behaviors are in the portfolio. If I can increase the size of the portfolio, I have created value.
- "What behavior can I implement next?" is more valuable the more the behaviors in that portfolio are valuable. I can't predict which behavior will be most valuable, nor how valuable it will be, but…
- I don't have to care which item will be most valuable, as long as I keep open the option of implementing it.
- (This is the best one.) The *more* uncertain my predictions of value are, the *greater* the value of the option is (versus just implementing it). If I embrace change, I maximize the value I create in exactly those situations where (then) conventional software development fails most spectacularly.

If you haven't encountered financial options before, here is my quick primer.

Start out with a thing with a price. A potato for a dollar. I have a dollar. You have a potato. I give you the dollar. You give me the potato. Now I have a potato, but I don't have the dollar. You have the dollar, but you don't have the potato anymore.

Maybe I don't want the potato now; I want it tomorrow. I'm sure will I want it tomorrow. I can give you a dollar today in return for your promise of a potato tomorrow. Tomorrow you deliver the potato, and we're both happy. I'll give you a little less than a dollar today, because of the time value of money.

What if I'm not sure if I want the potato tomorrow? I might have a picnic if the weather is good, in which case I'll make potato salad. If the weather is bad, though, I don't want to have bought a potato that will go to waste. In this case I can buy your promise of a potato tomorrow for a dollar tomorrow, but I might not hold you to that promise.

How much should I pay you for this "promise for a promise"? You're going to get the dollar tomorrow, but only if I hold you to your promise to sell your potato to me. You need to know what else you'll do with the potato if you can't sell it to me tomorrow. If you have other good uses for the potato tomorrow, then you can sell me this option for pennies. You don't much care if I buy it tomorrow or not. But if the potato is going to waste if I don't buy it tomorrow, then you have to charge me pretty much full price today.

I have just described a call option—the right, but not obligation, to purchase something in the future at a fixed price. Financial options have these parameters:

- The *underlying* thing that we can buy
- The *price* of the underlying, including the volatility of that price
- The *premium* of the option, or the price we pay today
- The *duration* of the option, or how long we have to decide whether to purchase the underlying (some options let you buy the underlying anytime between now and the end of the duration, which is what software looks like)

What does this mean for software design? Software design is preparation for change; change of behavior. The behavior changes we *could* make next are the potatoes from the story. Design we do today is the premium we pay for the "option" of "buying" the behavior change tomorrow.

Thinking of software design in terms of optionality turned my thinking upside-down. When I focused on balancing creating options and changing behavior, what used to scare me now excited me:

- The more volatile the value of a potential behavior change, the better.
- The longer I could develop, the better.
- Yes, the cheaper I could develop in future, the better, but that was a small proportion of the value.
- The less design work I could do to create an option, the better.

But I was still faced with that tricky problem I breezed over by saying, "Balancing creating options and changing behavior."

CHAPTER 27

Options Versus Cash Flows

Here we have the economic tug-of-war that makes "tidy first?" such an interesting question:

- Discounted cash flow tells us to make money sooner with greater likelihood and spend money later with less likelihood. Don't tidy first. That's spending money sooner and earning money later. Maybe don't even tidy after or later.

- Options tell us to spend money now to make more money later (even if we don't currently know exactly how). Absolutely tidy first (when it creates options). Tidy after and later too.

Tidy first? Yes. And also no.

Now, there are times to tidy first for sure. When:

cost(tidying) + cost(behavior change after tidying) < cost(behavior change without tidying)

then absolutely tidy first. It's still easy to get carried away and tidy too much, but set and maintain boundaries for how far you'll go and you'll be fine.

The more fraught situations occur when:

cost(tidying) + cost(behavior change after tidying) > cost(behavior change without tidying)

You might still want to tidy first, even though short-term economics discourage you. You may be implementing a series of behavior changes, all of which benefit from the tidying. Amortizing the cost of the tidying across all the changes might make sense, even discounting the cash flows.

Tidying first may make economic sense in spite of discounted cash flows if the value of the options created is greater than the value lost by spending money sooner and with certainty. We are firmly in the land of judgment here. Your sniffer might tell you,

"There's more good stuff here, but I need to tidy to be able to see it." That may be good enough evidence for more tidying.

Or, since software design is an exercise in human relationships and we're talking about our relationship with ourself at the scale of tidying, you might tidy first just because it makes the subsequent behavior changes more pleasant. A little bit of this "tidying as self-care" is justified. Just recognize that you are going counter to your economic incentives.

At the scale of tidying—minutes to hours—we can't (and shouldn't try to) precisely calculate the economics of our tidying. We are exercising two important forms of judgment, practicing for bigger things later:

- Getting used to being aware of the incentives affecting the timing and scope of software design ("I want to spend more time designing and I'm getting pushback. What's going on?")
- Practicing on ourselves the relationship skills that we will later be using with our direct colleagues, and then our more distant colleagues

Once we raise the stakes, where the survival and thrival of a product is on the line, we'll be glad of a gut sense of when and how to design and when not to design.

CHAPTER 28

Reversible Structure Changes

What's the difference between a bad haircut and a bad tattoo? The bad haircut grows out, but the bad tattoo is forever (well, not forever forever, but it's way harder to undo).

How are structure changes different from behavior changes? One property relevant to tidying first is that structure changes are generally reversible. You extract a helper function and you don't like it? Inline it. It's like that helper never existed.

Contrast this with a regrettable behavior change. Let's say you've sent out 100,000 tax notices with the wrong number on them. Now what? Well, it'll cost you plenty to fix them. The damage to your reputation may be permanent. If only you'd caught that problem five minutes *before* you sent the notices instead of five minutes *after*.

In general, we should treat reversible decisions differently than irreversible decisions. There's great value in reviewing, double-checking, triple-checking irreversible decisions. The pace should be slow and deliberate. Even if there is a great upside to the decision, there is also potentially a great downside if we get it wrong. Yes, we want the upside, but even more we want to avoid the downside.

How about reversible decisions? Most software design decisions are easily reversible. There is some upside to making them (making behavior changes easier, as we've seen throughout this book). But there's really not much downside, because we can so easily reverse a decision if it turns out to be wrong.

Because there is so little value to avoiding mistakes, we shouldn't invest much in doing so. That's the economic reality I was hinting at when choosing "tidying" to describe what we're doing in this book. It's no big deal. Just tidying.

Code review processes (which I've promised multiple times to trash, but now is not the time) don't distinguish between reversible and irreversible changes. We end up making the same investment with radically different payoff profiles. What a waste.

What about design changes that *aren't* reversible? For example, "extract as a service" tends to be a big deal and hard to undo. Think about it some more, for example by actually implementing a prototype first. And by "implementing," I mean putting it into production. Does this require a feature flag? Okay. Does it require checking the feature flag in a whole bunch of places? Okay, tidy first so it only requires a few feature flag checks.

Do you see what we're doing? We are making "extract as a service" reversible, at least for a while. If we get halfway into it and realize this is one of those services that really could have been a SQL query (thanks, Josh Wills), then we can change it without too much fuss.

Another scenario where reversible design decisions become irreversible is when the decision propagates throughout the code base. Now changing from an integer to a long would require changing a million spots, some of them extremely tricky. Okay: 1) think a little more about whether this decision is one that is likely to propagate, and 2) yeah that happens, and when it happens we get out of it one tidying at a time. Tidy first or after for a while, then tidy later to finish reversing the decision. (As always, in short, interruptible slices.)

There seems to be an idealistic form of geek thinking that holds that if only we made decisions better, we would never make mistakes. I was a young adherent, a worshipper at the altar of "If Only I Were Infinitely Smart." Fortunately, I got over it. I learned the value of reversibility (long before I had a name for it) and realized the value of making decisions reversible.

CHAPTER 29

Coupling

To prepare to write their classic text *Structured Design*, Ed Yourdon and Larry Constantine examined programs to find out what made them so expensive. They noticed that the expensive programs all had one property in common: changing one element required changing other elements. The cheap programs tended to require localized changes.

They dubbed this change infection property "coupling." Two elements are coupled with respect to a particular change if changing one element necessitates changing the other element.

For example, a calling function is coupled to a called function with respect to changes to the name of the called function:

```
caller()
    called()

called() // changing this name requires changing the call site(s) too
    ... // changing the formatting of the body requires no changes to call sites
```

The second comment here emphasizes an important nuance of coupling: we can't just say that two elements are coupled. To say something useful, we have to also say coupled with respect to which changes. If two elements are coupled with respect to a change that never happens, then they aren't coupled in a way that should concern us. That coupling is the boulder at the top of the hill that never rolls down to crush the village.

Analyzing coupling cannot be done simply by looking at the source code of a program. We need to know what changes have happened and/or are likely to happen before we can tell whether two elements are coupled. (For an experiment, see which pairs of files tend to show up together in commits. Those files are coupled.)

Coupling drives the cost of software. Because coupling is so fundamental, I express and visualize it in as many ways as I can. As a math-ish definition:

```
coupled(E1, E2, Δ) ≡ ΔE1 ⇒ ΔE2
```

Figure 29-1 shows this as an image.

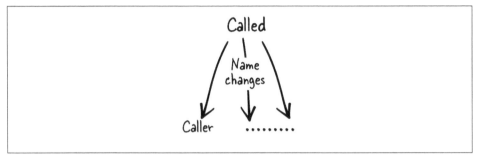

Figure 29-1. Called function coupled to calling function with respect to name changes

If coupling were only ever between two elements, then it wouldn't haunt our nightmares. Instead, coupling has two properties that drag it center stage:

1–N
> One element can be coupled with any number of other elements with respect to a change.

Cascading
> Once a change has rippled from one element to another, that implied change can trigger another round of changes, which can themselves trigger changes of their own.

The 1–N problem can be eliminated to some degree with tooling. If you have an automated refactoring to change a function name and all callers, then you can make a single change. The cost is the same whether you have one or one thousand callers. (Although if you're changing one thousand callers at once, you may want to get that change into production all by itself as quickly as possible.)

Cascading changes are the bigger issue. As we will see in the next book, the cost of changes follows a power law distribution. This distribution is created by the cost of cascading changes. You will be using software design to reduce the probability and magnitude of cascading changes.

The word "coupling" has lost its meaning over time, coming to mean any relationship between elements in a system. "This service is coupled with that service"—okay, but how? With respect to what changes? It's not enough to know that one service invokes another; we need to know what changes to one service would require changes to the other.

Meilir Page-Jones used the word "connascence" to describe coupling in his book *What Every Programmer Should Know About Object-Oriented Design* (Dorset House). Since the definitions are exactly the same, I just say "coupling."

In large, complex systems, coupling can be subtle. Indeed, when we say a system is "complex," we mean that changes have unexpected consequences. I remember an incident at Facebook where two services shared the same physical rack. One service changed its backup policy from incremental backups to complete backups. These backups saturated the network switch located on top of the rack, causing the second service to fail. The two services were coupled with respect to changes to the backup policy, even though the two teams working on the services weren't even aware of each other.

What does coupling mean for answering the question, "Should I tidy first?" Sometimes when you're staring at a messy change, it's coupling that's harshing your mellow: "But if I change this, then I'll have to change all those too." Messy. Take a minute to go through the list of tidyings and see which of them would reduce coupling.

Coupling drives the cost of software. Next, we'll look at exactly how.

CHAPTER 30

Constantine's Equivalence

I remember as a young programmer hearing dire reports that as much as 70% of software development costs went into maintenance. Seventy percent! How poor a job must we be doing that we make a thing and then have to spend twice as much just keeping it working?

Turns out that mental model of software, as a *thing* that is *made* and then should run forever unchanged, like some kind of perpetual motion machine, is the opposite of what really happens, and what *should* happen, too. The future value of a system reveals itself in today's realities, not yesterday's speculation.

With the way that coupling affects software development in place, we are ready to understand coupling's significance. In the original work on coupling and cohesion, *Structured Design*, Ed Yourdon and Larry Constantine postulated that the goal of software design is to minimize the cost of software (it's also to maximize the value, but we'll get to that). But what are those costs?

That 70% estimate turns out to be way too low. If we apply our creativity, we can release value-creating software after only a few percent of its eventual development cost. It's in everyone's best interest to do so. The sooner we get feedback from real usage, the less time/money/opportunity we spend on behavior that doesn't matter.

The first term of what I've dubbed "Constantine's Equivalence," then, is that the cost of software is approximately equal to the cost of changing it. Yes there is a brief period before we can be said to be "changing" it, but who cares? That period is economically insignificant. So:

    cost(software) ~= cost(change)

Another way to think about this is graphically. (What follows is not actual data, just another way to think about the problem. Adjust accordingly.)

If we graph the cumulative cost of software over its lifespan, we get something like a logistic curve (Figure 30-1). The period before release represents both a small portion of the total time and a small portion of the total cost.

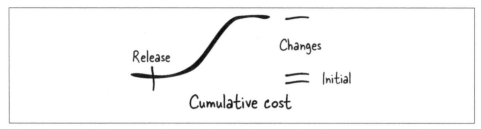

Figure 30-1. Logistic curve of cumulative cost showing that changes are most of the expense

What can we say about the cost of change? Are all changes equal? Of course not, not if I ask the question like that. We can bump along making small changes to the behavior of the system, all of them costing about the same. Then one day we make a change superficially similar to all the previous changes, but this one blows up in our faces. Instead of costing one unit, it costs ten or a hundred or a thousand.

Visualized, the cost per month (say) starts low, grows rapidly, then shrinks as other opportunities become more profitable (Figure 30-2). But why is the slope of cost growth so much steeper after release? Are we really making more changes? Yes, some more. But also, the existing system has started to create friction. We have to worry about backward compatibility. We have to worry about production stability. We have to worry about all the ways any one change might break seemingly unrelated features.

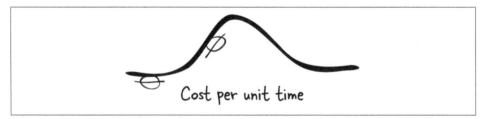

Figure 30-2. Cost per time grows slowly, then rapidly, then shrinks

If you know about power law distributions, you recognize what's going on here (if you don't know about power law distributions, please be careful, because I ended up obsessed by them for 20 years). One characteristic of power law distributions is that the few big "outlier" events matter a lot. Add them up and they outweigh the far more numerous "normal" events. The five biggest storms cause more damage than ten thousand small storms.

Is this sounding familiar? The most expensive behavior changes cost, together, far more than all the least expensive behavior changes put together. Put another way, the cost of change is approximately equal to the cost of the big changes:

```
cost(change) ~= cost(big changes)
```

What makes those expensive changes expensive? It's when changing this element requires changing those two elements, each of which requires changing other elements, and… and… and…. What "propagates" change? Coupling. So, the cost of software is approximately equal to the coupling:

```
cost(big changes) ~= coupling
```

And now we have the full Constantine's Equivalence:

```
cost(software) ~= cost(change) ~= cost(big changes) ~= coupling
```

Or, to highlight the importance of software design:

```
cost(software) ~= coupling
```

To reduce the cost of software, we must reduce coupling. But decoupling isn't free and is subject to trade-offs, which we explore next.

CHAPTER 31

Coupling Versus Decoupling

Why don't you just decouple all the things? Why have any coupling at all?

Coupling, like the Lego piece in the night, often isn't obvious until you step on it. You go to make a behavior change, then notice, "Oh, if I change this, I will have to change that, and that too." Or worse, you change this, put it in production, break things, and realize, "Oh, I guess I also have to change that and that." You're not aware what unconscious assumptions you're making.

Discounted cash flows account for some coupling. There's a quick, coupled way to implement some behavior, and a longer, more expensive, decoupled way. At the time, you made the economically correct decision to implement it with coupling—revenue sooner, expenses later. Now it's later.

Another legitimate reason to have coupling in a system is because it wasn't a problem until just now. The boulder that was perched on the hill decided now was a good time to roll down. "Who knew that we would have to translate this into any other language?" And you didn't. Until you did.

A final reason to have coupling is that some coupling is just inevitable. I'm afraid I don't have a better argument for this than "confident assertion." I'll work on it.

It doesn't really matter why the coupling is there. You're faced with a choice today: pay the cost of coupling or pay the cost of decoupling. "Tidy first?" is this decision in miniature (although only some messes are made of coupling).

Let's take a look at a concrete example—a communication protocol. A simple way to implement it is to have a sending function and a receiving function:

```
Sender>>send()
    writeField1()
    writeField2()

Receiver>>receive()
    readField1()
    readField2()
```

These functions are coupled. Change one, and you'd better change the other. Then you have to worry about deploying the changes in perfect synchronization.

By the hundredth time you modify these functions, you're probably getting tired of the extra care required. You define an interface definition language:

```
format = [
    {field: "1", type: "integer"},
    {field: "2", type: "string"}
]

Sender>>send()
    writeFields(format)

Receiver>>receive()
    readFields(format)
```

Poof! Coupling gone. Now you can change the format in one place. No need to change send() and receive() at the same time.

But it turns out the coupling isn't "gone" gone. Yes, we can change the format in one place, say by adding a third field. However, somewhere deep inside the Sender, we still need to compute that third field. Until we've done that, we can't read and use the field in the Receiver. So Sender and Receiver are still coupled; if Receiver needs to change to use the new field, Sender needs to change too. We have given ourself more options for the order of implementation.

Here's something I believe but can't prove or adequately explain: the more you reduce coupling for one class of changes, the greater the coupling becomes for other classes of changes. The practical implication of this (if it matches your intuition) is that you shouldn't bother to squeeze out every last bit of coupling. The coupling created in doing so isn't worth it.

Overall, we are left with a trade-off space (Figure 31-1).

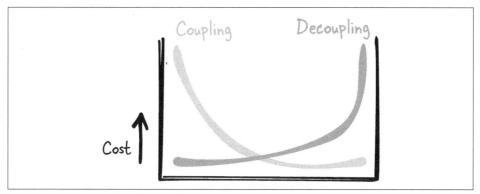

Figure 31-1. Cost of coupling trades off with cost of decoupling

This picture is naive in that the exact costs of coupling and decoupling aren't knowable in advance. These costs both play out over time, which introduces discounted cash flows. Decoupling also creates options, the value of which is uncertain and evolves over time.

The fundamental decision space remains. You can pay the cost of coupling or pay the cost (and reap the benefits) of decoupling. And you can fall anywhere along this continuum. No wonder software design is hard. And we won't even get to the interpersonal relationship part until the next book in this series.

CHAPTER 32

Cohesion

Coupled elements should be subelements of the same containing element. That's the first implication of cohesion. Shovel all the manure into one pile. The second implication of cohesion is that elements that aren't manure (well, that aren't coupled) should go elsewhere.

For example, suppose we have a module containing 10 functions. Three of those functions are coupled. Where do the other seven go? We have two options (Figure 32-1).

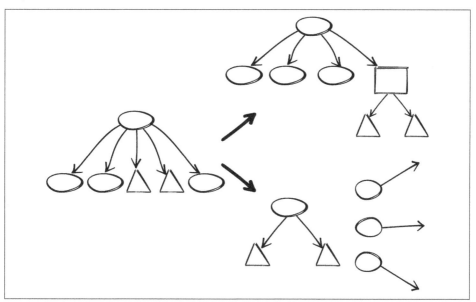

Figure 32-1. Incohesive element improved either by (top) extracting a cohesive subelement or by (bottom) moving uncoupled subelements elsewhere

The first is to bundle the coupled elements into their own subelement. We could create a submodule that only contained the three functions. That submodule would be cohesive because its elements were coupled. The original module might be less cohesive because now none of its elements would be coupled, but we won't be in worse shape than before.

Extracting a helper function is this kind of "extract a cohesive subelement" approach. If the lines of the helper function have to be changed together, then the helper is cohesive, with all the benefits that come from cohesion: easier analysis, easier change, resistance to accidental behavior change.

The second option is to take the uncoupled elements and put them elsewhere. Where? This is where you get to be a designer. What are those functions coupled with? Move the functions closer to their siblings. Are they coupled with each other? Make another submodule for them to live in.

Make no sudden moves. You're working with incomplete and changing information about what's coupled with what. Don't dramatically rearrange everything. Move one element at a time. Make the code tidier for the next person. If everyone follows the Scout rule ("leave it better than you found it"), the code will become more livable-with over time.

CHAPTER 33

Conclusion

And with that you are prepared to answer the question "tidy first?" Over and over. Each time slightly differently, but each time affected by the same forces:

- Cost—Will tidying make costs smaller, later, or less likely?
- Revenue—Will tidying make revenue larger, sooner, or more likely?
- Coupling—Will tidying make it so I need to change fewer elements?
- Cohesion—Will tidying make it so the elements I need to change are in a smaller, more concentrated scope?

Most important, though, is you. Will tidying bring peace, satisfaction, and joy to your programming? Maybe some. This is important because if you are your best self, you are a better programmer. You can't be your best self if you're always rushing, if you're always changing code that's painful to change.

Don't get carried away with tidying. Once you realize you can make your own life and work better by tidying, sometimes and somewhat, you can get giddy. Unlike the risk and uncertainty of features, where you can do what you think is right and folks can still be dissatisfied, you are the audience for your tidying, and you're very likely to be satisfied.

Coupling conducts one tidying to the next to the next. Tidyings are the Pringles of software design. When you're tidying first, resist the urge to eat the next one. Tidy to enable the next behavior change. Save the tidying binge for later, when you can go nuts without delaying the change someone else is waiting for.

And be aware that as you practice tidying for yourself, you are preparing to design on behalf of others like you. That's where this is going—making software design an ordinary, balanced part of development.

We seldom program alone. Just as there is coupling between elements in a design, we are coupled to each other. A change I make can ripple to you, and a change you make can ripple to me.

This first book has dealt with software design by and for individuals. Sure, your colleagues will benefit from tidier code, but the focus has been on you. Is it worth some investment to help you work with greater ease? Probably.

Who?	When?	What?	How?	Why?
You	Minutes to hours	Tidyings	SB diffs	Coupling and cohesion

The next book in the series examines the relationships between changers, those who can directly change the system. We must get those relationships healthy before we are prepared for the ultimate relationship challenge, between changers and those who can do little but wait for our changes to land. Software design can nourish these relationships or damage them.

Who?	When?	What?	How?	Why?
You	Minutes to hours	Tidyings	SB diffs	Coupling and cohesion
You and programmer colleagues	Days to weeks	Refactorings	Weekly planning	Power laws

Of all people, I know not to plan too far ahead, but the ultimate payoff of this brilliant technique you are learning is to get along better with people who aren't like you. The relationships between business-oriented folks and technology-oriented folks are the most fraught, but also the most consequential and potentially the most rewarding. Once you make software design part of both daily business and strategic planning, you have the opportunity to play your part in healing the rift between business and technology.

Who?	When?	What?	How?	Why?
You	Minutes to hours	Tidyings	SB diffs	Coupling and cohesion
You and programmer colleagues	Days to weeks	Refactorings	Weekly planning	Power laws
All stakeholders	Months to years	Architectural evolution	Dynamic balance	?

That's where we're going with this—to make software design truly an exercise in human relationships. So to start…

Tidy first? Likely yes. Just enough. You're worth it.

Annotated Reading List and References

Alexander, Christopher. *Notes on the Synthesis of Form*. Cambridge: Harvard University Press, 1964.

> The book that introduced patterns. The basic idea is that each design decision resolves some of the conflicting constraints and creates (one hopes smaller) constraints to be resolved by future decisions. These configurations of constraints repeat, hence the word "pattern."

---. *The Timeless Way of Building*. New York: Oxford University Press, 1979.

> I can't recommend this book highly enough. It starts by re-imagining the relationship between designers and those designed for. Who should have the power to do what? It then applies patterns and novel construction techniques to defer most design decisions far beyond what would seem sensible (is this sounding familiar yet?).

Ball, Philip. *Branches: Nature's Patterns*. New York: Oxford University Press, 2011.

---. *Flow: Nature's Patterns*. New York: Oxford University Press, 2011.

---. *Shapes: Nature's Patterns*. New York: Oxford University Press, 2011.

> As designers of an intellectual artifact, we tend to believe that we can design whatever we want however we want to design it. Nope. Our work is subject to natural laws (more about this in the next *Empirical Software Design* book). This trilogy is a cabinet of curiosities from design in the natural world.

Beck, Kent. *Smalltalk Best Practice Patterns*. New York: Pearson Education, 1997.

---. *Implementation Patterns*. Upper Saddle River: Addison-Wesley, 2007.

> These two books address design at the scale addressed by *Tidy First?*. The question answered is, "How would we code if we wanted to communicate with other humans?"

Feathers, Michael. *Working Effectively with Legacy Code*. Upper Saddle River: Pearson Education, 2004.

> An inspiring take on continuing to design in spite of the constraints created by legacy and production code.

Fowler, Martin. *Refactoring: Improving the Design of Existing Code*. Boston: Addison-Wesley, 1999.

> A handbook of ways to improve existing designs.

Hanson, Chris, and Gerald Jay Sussman. *Software Design for Flexibility*. Cambridge: MIT Press, 2021.

> Small-scale design approaches that tend to support ongoing change.

Lemaire, Maude. *Refactoring at Scale*. Sebastopol: O'Reilly Media, 2021.

> This book resolves the often-conflicting constraints of new features, better structure, and the need for reliable production.

Mollison, B.C. *Permaculture 1*. London: Transworld Publishers, 1988.

> My definition of design as "beneficially relating elements" restates the definition of permaculture. Permaculture is a discipline of designing ecosystems that yield value while retaining the resilience of natural ecosystems.

Myers, Glenford J. *Composite/Structured Design*. New York: Van Nostrand Reinhold, 1978.

> An early approach to information hiding—functions in modules that assume as little about each other as possible.

Norman, Don. *The Design of Everyday Things*. New York: Basic Books, 2013.

> You'll never again blame yourself for pulling a door instead of pushing it. Also, the "affordances" Don describes are applicable to software design.

Normand, Eric. *Grokking Simplicity*. Shelter Island: Manning, 2021.

> Some folks think it's "functions versus objects." I agree with Eric that the more valuable perspective is "functions inside objects." This book addresses the cost of change by applying functional programming.

Ousterhout, John. *A Philosophy of Software Design*. Palo Alto: Yaknyam Press, 2018.

> This is the book that got me off my butt writing. John's points are well taken about making design better, but they are presented dogmatically—always keep your code as clean as you possibly can. The question mark in *Tidy First?* is a direct response.

Page-Jones, Meilir. *What Every Programmer Should Know About Object-Oriented Design*. New York: Dorset House, 1995.

> A translation of coupling into the world of objects. Since the definitions of "coupling" and "connascence" are identical, I use "coupling."

Parnas, David Lorges. *Software Fundamentals: Collected Papers by David L. Parnas*. Edited by Daniel M. Hoffman and David M. Weiss. Boston: Addison-Wesley Professional, 2001.

> Professor Parnas knew about design before pretty much everyone. His thinking and vocabulary shape our conversations.

Petre, Marian, and Andre Van Der Hoek. *Software Design Decoded*. Cambridge: MIT Press, 2016.

> Describes activities you'll see expert designers apply. Since it's such a short, approachable book, there is little detail about any given activity. Use it as a prompt: "Well, I don't ever do *that*, so I'd better try it."

Seemann, Mark. *Code That Fits in Your Head*. Boston: Addison-Wesley Professional, 2021.

> The human brain doesn't come with an operator's manual. This book is close to an operator's manual for the programming brain.

Weinberg, Gerald M. *The Psychology of Computer Programming*. New York: Dorset House, 1998.

> The book that pioneered the radical approach of assuming programmers are humans.

Yourdon, Edward. *Techniques of Program Structure and Design*. Upper Saddle River: Prentice Hall, 1975.

An early description of software design, superseded by…

Yourdon, Edward, and Larry L. Constantine. *Structured Design*. Upper Saddle River: Prentice Hall, 1979.

This is the bible of software design. Newton's laws for software designers. Everything in *Tidy First?* restates points made in *Structured Design*.

Index

B

batches
    behavior changes and, 43
    costs, 44-45
    Goldilocks dilemma, 43
    trade-off space, 43
behavior
    options and, 70
    structure and, 61-63
    value and, 61
behavior changes, 35-37, 43
    clustering, 48
beneficially relating elements, 57-59

C

cascading changes, 78
cash flow, 73-74
    coupling and, 85
chaining, 39
    chunk statements and, 40
    cohesion order and, 40
    comments, 41
        redundant, 41
    dead code and, 39
    explaining constants and, 40
    explaining variables and, 40
    explicit parameters and, 40
    extract helper, 40
    guard clauses and, 39
    interfaces, 39
    One Pile and, 40
    reading order and, 40
changers, 92
chunk statements, 23

chaining and, 40
chunking statements, 36
clauses, guard clauses, 3-4
cohesion, 89-90
cohesion order, 13
    chaining and, 40
comments
    chaining and, 41
    headers, 29
    redundant, deleting, 31-32, 41
connascence, 79
Constantine's Equivalence, 81-83
constants
    explaining, chaining and, 40
    literal, 19
coupling, 77-79
    discounted cash flows, 85
    software development and, 81
    versus decoupling, 85-87

D

dead code, 5
    chaining and, 39
decisions, reversible, 75-76
declaring variables, 15-16
decoupling, 13, 85-87
dependencies, 16
discounted cash flows, coupling and, 85

E

elements
    beneficially relating elements, 57-59
    boundaries, 57
    cohesion, 90

U

untangling tidyings, 49-50

V

value, behavior and, 61
valuing software system, 67-68

variables
    declaration, 15-16
    explaining, chaining and, 40
    expressions, 17
    initialization, 15-16
    lazily initialized, 7

About the Author

Kent Beck is a programmer, creator of Extreme Programming, pioneer of software patterns, coauthor of JUnit, rediscoverer of Test-Driven Development, and observer of 3X: Explore/Expand/Extract. Beck is also alphabetically the first signatory of the Agile Manifesto. He lives in San Francisco, California, and he is Chief Scientist at Mechanical Orchard, teaching skills to help geeks feel safe in the world.

Readers can connect with or follow him via:

- Facebook: *https://www.facebook.com/kentlbeck*
- Twitter: *https://twitter.com/KentBeck*
- LinkedIn: *https://www.linkedin.com/in/kentbeck*
- Medium: *https://medium.com/@kentbeck_7670*
- Website: *https://www.kentbeck.com*

Colophon

The animal on the cover of *Tidy First?* is a Maine Coon *(Felis catus)*, the official state cat of Maine and one of the largest and oldest domesticated cat breeds.

Maine Coons are known for their impressive size and fluffy fur; males typically weigh between 13 and 18 pounds, while females range from 8 to 12 pounds. They have a robust and muscular body with their characteristic long, bushy tail and tufted lynx-like ears. Maine Coons have striking gold, green, or copper eyes.

Their fur is dense, water-resistant, and comes in a wide range of colors and patterns such as black, white, cream, and various shades of brown, with tabby or tortoiseshell designs. Due to their thick fur, Maine Coons require regular grooming, especially during shedding seasons, to prevent matting.

These cats are renowned for their affectionate and sociable nature. They are known to be good with children and other cats and dogs, making them excellent family companions. Their playful and intelligent nature makes them quick learners and they can be taught tricks and games. They have a fondness for interactive toys and enjoy activities that stimulate their minds.

Many of the animals on O'Reilly covers are endangered; all of them are important to the world.

The cover illustration is by Karen Montgomery, based on an antique line engraving from Dover's *Animals*. The cover fonts are Gilroy Semibold and Guardian Sans. The text font is Adobe Minion Pro; the heading font is Adobe Myriad Condensed; and the code font is Dalton Maag's Ubuntu Mono.

O'REILLY®

Learn from experts.
Become one yourself.

Books | Live online courses
Instant answers | Virtual events
Videos | Interactive learning

Get started at oreilly.com.

Printed in the USA
CPSIA information can be obtained
at www.ICGtesting.com
JSHW060728160424
61205JS00011BA/564

9 781098 151249